THE ......
OF KABUL

THE BANDIT OF KABUL

EPISODE TWO OF THE SERIES:
As the Prayer Wheel Turns

by

Jerry Beisler

REGENT PRESS
Oakland, California
2006

ISBN 13: 978-1-58790-094-5
ISBN 10: 1-58790-094-7
LCCN: 2006927993

Book Design & Production
Mark Weiman

Manufactured in the United States of America
REGENT PRESS
Berkeley, California
www.regentpress.net

"Most writers regard the truth as their most valuable possession,
and therefore are most economical in its use."
Mark Twain

"Be the change you wish to see in the world."
Mahatma Gandhi

"Throw the peace sign in the air and say 'higher' —
it'll do you no harm."
Sly of "Sly and the Family Stone" to the crowd at Woodstock

"It's better to have weed in the time of no money
than money in the time of no weed."
Free Wheelin' Franklin

"You're the party, the Grateful Dead is the excuse."
Jerry Garcia

"Don't get the idea that I'm knocking the American system."
Al Capone

"I got forty red, white and blue shoe strings and a thousand
telephones that don't ring.
Do you know where I can get rid of these things?"
"Highway 61 Revisited," Bob Dylan

"Smoking is a custom, loathsome to the eye, hateful to the nose,
harmful to the brain, dangerous to the lungs, and in the black,
stinking fumes thereof, nearest resembles the horrible Stygian
smoke of the pit that is bottomless."
"On Smoking," by King James, 1604 A.D.

"All of a sudden I could hear somebody whistling from right
behind me. I turned and she said 'Why do you always end up
down at Nick's café?' I said 'I don't know, the wind
just kind of pushed me this way.'"
"Somewhere Down the Crazy River," Robbie Robertson

"The only thing new is the history you just learned."
Harry Truman

.

Prologue / Author's Note

This book is set in some of the world's most remote and exotic locations, but you will not be reading poetic or minute descriptions of the sights, sounds or smells of those places. There are no carefully crafted remembrances of deeply emotional interludes, frighteningly fearful experiences or moments of ecstatic joy, though they did, naturally, occur. Nor will love, in all its many aspects and facets, be inspected, analyzed or remembered in detail. There is no time for dwelling on these things during this era of endless war that produces murderous national leaders, idiotic economic policies and draconian, tyrannical laws. But the historical facts, the action and adventure, the spirit and spirituality of human beings are here; this story begins and ends with love.

Chapter One

"If it didn't happen this way, it should have."

Goa, India, was hyped as the counter-culture Nirvana. If the hippies ran Disneyland, it would be a lot like Goa – with sex, some herb to smoke and the greatest mango lassies you ever tasted. It would be real life, not the plastic, future-modern society that stifles freedom with conformity and bourgeois boredom.

The pirates that preyed on cargo traffic out of hidden coves that lined the Goa coast were not the "Pirates of the Caribbean," an amusement park attraction acted out by human manikins, but were real pirates and there the differences begin.

In fact, Goa was anything but what the traveling, hippie-community exaggeration of paradise was said to be. The first night that my fiancée, Rebecca, and I arrived, we missed our creature comforts and we learned what the real definition of "creature" comfort is.

Sleeping on the hard wooden slats that passed for a bed, to the accompanying buzz of mosquitoes eagerly feasting upon us two American delights, caused us to have a few moments of doubt about our proposed stay.

Rebecca and I found the house with the heart on the roof the next day. It was one of only three structures on the entire 50 miles of beach that had the benefit of intermittent electricity. We

discovered that padded mattresses were available from local merchants as were colorful fabrics to use for bedding or beach wear.
A mosquito net provided the necessary protection from our buzz-
ing, blood-besotted friends. The alternative was a coil of reeking
incense, probably laced with DDT.

The farmer's market consensus was that a couple of hundred
people lived on the beaches from Calengute to Anjuna. The local
populace survived off fishing and were happy with the low-key
commerce these international types contributed to their villages.

Our next-door neighbors were Shashi and Jennifer Kapoor
and their two young sons. The Kapoors were definitely not hippies
and while not opposed to the lifestyle, were strongly anti-drug,

especially in front of
their children. Shashi
was a third-genera-
tion actor related to a
long line of Bollywood
producers, directors
and promoters. Jen-
nifer, Shashi's lovely, blonde English wife, boasted of parents who
were Shakespearean actors during the period of the English Raj
and who had remained in India. Now, in the retirement age of
their lives, Jennifer's parents continued to perform two-person
Shakespearean plays.

Shashi was notified, by telegram, of his starring role in
producer/director Conrad Rooks film "Siddhartha" a week after we
met them. He and Jennifer and the children were elated and had a
small, celebratory party when they shared the news with us.

The beaches of Goa were spectacular, a seemingly endless
span of sand and palm trees. The waters of the Arabian Sea were
not particularly beautiful, being somewhat murky and filled with
small sharks. All the same, we enjoyed a couple of swims every
day. Evenings would find us strolling along, enjoying the sunset
and admiring the waves lining the shore with glittering, phospho-

rescent streaks.

Conversely, one of the more charming aspects of Goa was the sanitary system. All houses came complete with a convenient out-house that was backed up against a pig pen and raised above the area that the pigs inhabited by three steps. When one used the facilities, little snouts would be visible at the end of the shoot, grunting eagerly while awaiting their morning breakfast. The pigs became our constant companions on treks to these out-houses. Watching them scurry for the choicest spot at the end of the plumping shoot caused us to realize how the term "piggy back" may have originated. Nevertheless, once we moved into our charming little home with the heart on the roof, mosquito nets in place to protect us and softer bedding for indulging in topical lust, the days and nights became much more pleasant in the land of Goa.

Daily life in Goa included one Father Perez, the last Catholic priest left in the former Portuguese colony. Kicked out of the subcontinent at gun point in 1964 by the Indian government, all that remained of the colonists was the traditional Portuguese sweetbread that we had enjoyed, and the one Catholic Church managed by Father Perez on four rupees a day. Father Perez was either admired or despised by the traveling community. He made a living changing money on the black market for the foreigners and would of-

Rebecca and our friend Father Perez

After the party

ten drop by our house with his own coconut chillum contraption and mooch a little hashish to smoke. He was known to have had postcards made up of himself standing in front of a gaggle of young Hindi boys. He sent these postcards to unsuspecting suckers asking them for donations to support a fictional soccer team. Father Perez spent hours recounting, always with great laughter, his threats to the Hindi wives of local fishermen. After their husbands sailed out to sea for the daily fishing expedition, Father Perez would intimidate the wives with impending evil spells if they didn't give him money.

Attracted to these beaches was a parade of characters from all over the world. Being frequent guests at Joe Banana's Fruit Shake shop and "Tony's Up the Beach" we joined the international throng dining on seafood and the simple, local fare. The relaxed, jovial atmosphere made it seem to us that the cream of the traveling community had found their way to Goa. Artists came with portfolios of their original work and decorated many of the houses with murals. The musically talented played exotic instruments such as the sitar, oud and vina, and the not-so-exotic guitars, drums and flutes. Spontaneous music was a daily occurrence on the porches of hippie houses. Writers, searching for perfect metaphors for a brand new scene, sent letters and articles to their far

flung families, friends and homeland media, chronicling the hap-
penings and high jinks in Goa and beyond. These original hippies
created a swirling, mesmerizing cacophony of sound and color.
Getting into the spirit of things, Rebecca and I enjoyed psilocy-
bin one full-moon night. It added more magic and romance to an
experience already in a timeless, primal setting with a feeling of
human oneness. Goa.

For Christmas we decided to throw a party. Rebecca had
purchased a gallon of Canadian maple syrup at a duty-free shop
on our way to India. It inspired me to use the local Portuguese

Shark boats on Christmas day.

Jerry

Eight Finger Eddy

Montreal Michael

Photos by Rebecca

sweetbread and readily available eggs for French toast. Before Christmas morning I hired four Goanese women to chop up a variety of fruits and make huge fruit salads. We produced a unique, welcome feast for about 200 people, including Peace Corps volunteers and other travelers who heard about the party by coconut telegraph up and down the beach from as far as 50 miles away.

As the party cranked into full gear, a group spontaneously decided to rent three canoe-style outriggers from the local shark fishermen. This turned out to be a much more exciting adventure than first thought. After piling a half-dozen sated and stoned party-goers into the boats, and clearing the shore break, we found ourselves cruising festively in open water. The fishermen then proceeded to set up for themselves several bottles of an illegal, powerful whiskey and launched into a celebration of their own. Gleeful at their unexpected, over-paid rental success, they swilled liquor until they were blind drunk. These outriggers were very narrow and no one had experience in manning such a craft – our lives were given over to the more and more inebriated, celebrating fishermen. It was with great difficulty that we managed, by hand signals and body language, to instruct them to row us ashore at Chapora Beach for a swim. After a relaxing, enjoyable dip and a few hits off the chillum, it was then up to us to pile the besotted fishermen, now asleep, back into the boats and launch ourselves and the other fools towards our home beach – in the darkness, through shark-filled waters. When we finally hit the beach at our Heart House, the party was still raging and would do so all night long.

As the days flowed together in the month that we spent in Goa, it became obvious that the primitive living conditions were putting an unhealthy stress on everyone's lifestyle. Foolish hippies were eating something called Mandrax, a form of Quaalude, just to get them through the nights. Smoking prodigious amounts of hashish all day long was a common pastime. More acid arrived when members of the Brotherhood of Light from Southern California

came upon the scene. Girls went topless on the beach and men
wore nothing but the g-string type bathing suit preferred by the
local fishermen. The local women bathed in full saris and seemed
not to mind that their scantily clad foreign sisters were bouncing
around the beach. This fantastic feeling of "freedom found" was
compromised by the primitive lifestyle and the spread of lice and
disease. The time to move on was quickly approaching.

It was in Goa that I connected with a Canadian we called
Montreal Michael. Michael came up with the concept of extracting
oil from hashish in an ingenious way to slide it past unsuspecting customs agents. Michael's "bonafides" to me were his 20 or
more heavy textbooks, U.N. Reports and scientific journals that
he referred to as a "study library." His mother had been a member
of the LeDain Commission created by the Canadian Government
to study and present recommendations to the progressive Prime
Minister, the worldly Pierre Trudeau. The commissioners voted
five to four against legalization in their report. Michael inherited
the "study library" his mother had used in her academic examination of the history and use of cannabis. Michael had hauled these
heavy books to this center of low-key hedonism more replete with
paperback novels than texts. He told me that he was going to go
to Afghanistan and try and put the extraction operation together.
I said I was planning to make a trip to Afghanistan as well for the
major, ultimate horseback ride of my life and that if I saw him
there I'd consider taking a look at his idea. We talked about a plan
to transport hashish from legal Nepal and Afghanistan to quasi-
legal Amsterdam. If only the countries in between didn't carry a
sentence of ten years of hard prison if caught. We never shared
these thoughts or plans with Rebecca. She had little use for legal
subtleties.

Shashi Kapoor departed for Bombay to begin filming "Siddhartha." We found ourselves spending more quality time with
Jennifer and the children rather than the hippies who found their
way to our front porch and who mostly wanted to talk of their acid

trips the night before. It was at this time that I made a cardinal rule in my traveler's life: no stories about acid trips. Boring. What was not boring, however, was the whisper of war between India and Pakistan.

Most people arrived in and departed from Goa on large, cargo-carrying ferry boats that plied their trade along the shore to Bombay and back. On the way down from Bombay the boat would moor a half-mile from shore and it was fascinating to see the small boats rowing out to collect the various supplies that were, in many instances, just tossed overboard into the waiting vessels.

The ferry did have six lovely first-class cabins on the upper deck, which we had the foresight to book round trip.

We left Goa in January with our sights on Nepal and the beginning of an import business. Jennifer Kapoor and her two children joined us on the ferry. The lower deck was filled with hippies heading back towards the hashish trail, replaced by those pouring into the hippie Disneyland.

Rebecca and I were so overcome by the romance of our journey that we decided to be married by the ship's Captain, an event reminiscent of those classic seafaring ceremonies of yore.

In the spirit of occasion Jennifer Kapoor went below and commandeered, as she said, "the best looking European Don Juan I could find."

He was Alejandro, a handsome Spaniard whom Rebecca and I had met at various Goa celebrations. Unfortunately he could not be the best man and stand up at the wedding because he was so inebriated he could not stand. We propped Alejandro against the life ring and Jennifer Kapoor accompanied Rebecca as maid of honor. The first mate was my best man. The brief rite was held on the open deck and highlighted by a beautiful, gigantic red sun setting into the Arabian Sea behind us.

The Captain entered our marriage into the ship's log.

Chapter Two

"Hark, now hear the sailors cry
Smell the sea and feel the sky
Let your soul and spirit fly into the mystic."
"INTO THE MYSTIC," VAN MORRISON

A threat of war hissed through Bombay. The world powers had ludicrously allowed the creation of an East and West Pakistan with thousands of square miles of India in between.

We checked into the Ambassador Hotel, then went to fight the lines to buy railroad tickets "towards Kathmandu."

Everything got hazy that first night in Bombay. We ran into our would-be best man, Alejandro, and he asked us if we had ever been to an opium parlor. "Your honeymoon night in Bombay . . . why not?"

"We go to 'vice' part of the city. Anything goes . . . for centuries," Alejandro emphasized, "for centuries!" Alejandro further explained that "the deal was to visit the O dens in the Sokologie Square part of Bombay but, above all, to avoid spending many days there."

"Come, I'll take you down there," he said "and we must go now and you must start to say the following mantra: 'I will not stay more than 8 hours, I will not stay more than 8 hours' because the masters of the pipe will continue to offer to refill your pipe until there is no money left. Some people have actually started to get their mail there," he further cautioned.

"We're headed to the mountains and safety tomorrow," we

Alejandro

replied in unison.

When we entered the opium den we caused quite a stir. Seeing a beautiful blonde woman such as Rebecca always caught some local attention. The docents of the den spread new newspaper on the floor and gave us a tin can for a pillow. Squatting next to us and filling the long opium pipe with small balls of "O," these den walas instructed us to take big, full drags on the pipe. Like every drug in my experience, the first-time use is the best-time use and I was quickly transported to blue lagoons, red sails and golden sunrises. We were offered tea and soft drinks and, of course, many opportunities to refill our pipes. Now and then the Alejandro warning – "no more than 8 hours" – would occasionally bounce cross the bucolic scenery that I was enjoying in my head. Rebecca and I agreed it was time to go. Alejandro refused and we left.

We were astonished to find ourselves greeted by a brand new day – It was six in the morning and the city of Bombay was rocking. We walked into the breaking day across the Square and saw thousands of prostitutes stacked in tiny cages six stories high in building after building. Everywhere small cooking fires shed an eerie glow on the teaming populace, each soul eking out a bitter survival in scenes that rivaled everything I recalled from reading "Dante's Inferno." We could not have been farther from our small, conservative, hometowns. It felt as if I had just looked into a strange mirror. Everything looks back at you differently. I had walked through a door of perception. A time shift. The teaming masses of Asia were now a "reality."

We missed the train and awoke after twenty-four hours of delirium to receive humankind's most horrific notice of reality. India and Pakistan were at war. Bombay was under blackout with the threat of Pakistani air force bombing. The entire populace seemed to be in a wild, patriotic panic. Lawlessness and civil chaos were breaking out in the streets. Bombay was within striking distance of the Pakistani air force and all seaports and airports were closed. The only safe move was inland, and fast.

Chapter Three

"If you smile at me you, know I will understand
'Cause that is something everybody everywhere does
In the same language."
"WOODEN SHIPS," STILLS, CROSBY & KANTNER

Tight, white, starched collared shirts, turbans, dhotis and Levis pushed and paid to get on the Delhi Mail and hopefully get out of artillery range and death from above. An expired ticket and a bag full of rupees got us on the train.

Any seasoned traveler during that era will tell you that the best part of discovering India was the rail system. Created by the British during their Raj Empire, railroads still employed mostly Sikhs as engineers and station managers. They ran the train system to perfection and to the minute. It was always unbelievable to newcomers that one could schedule a train trip across thousands of miles of India, a country where nothing – I repeat nothing – worked and find, surprisingly, that the trains showed up nearly to the minute. Then you found your little name card placed neatly on the door to your cabin and discovered savory food and pleasant service awaited you from employees who truly appreciated their jobs as did the most elite in the country.

Our first train trip was not nearly so posh. We were two of twelve, emitting excessive body odor from nervous fear and the speculative scramble to board, in a four-person cabin. Rebecca and I were forced off the train when it was commandeered by soldiers for the war effort at Allahabad. We were very fortunate to find accommodation in a hotel owned by a local family revered for generations as classical musicians. The war ended and with it the constant tension everyone was experiencing. We left the confines of the hotel grounds and ventured into the central market. This led to a bizarre experience of human interaction in a Muslim jewelry shop in the Allahabad souk. Rebecca and I drew a crowd of hundreds, pressing and milling outside the jewelry shop. Every minute or two one of the young nephews of the store's owner grabbed a cat-o-nine-tails and ran yelling and screaming and slashing into the pulsing throng and beat them away from the door. Within moments the crowd began to form again to watch the blonde Western woman. The shop owner's volatile young toughs would again grab the cat-o-nine-tails and race out of the building flailing madly. "Taxi please" and thanks to all for pounding on the fenders and windows, too!

The international media reported a million dead and the creation of the new nation of Bangladesh. Mercifully and fortunately the war was brief. The truce allowed us to get a first-class train cabin to Agra. One of the propaganda tools that the Indians effectively used to rile up the population in the war effort was to broadcast that the Pakistanis were trying, daily, to bomb the Taj Mahal. The propaganda would turn out to be beneficial to us since there were virtually no tourists in Agra, home of the Taj Mahal. Not only did we get our choice of the finest room in the finest hotel but, for a small fee, we were

allowed into the Taj Mahal, alone, at night. On two consecutive evenings, under the dome of the Taj with our Tibetan bells and bowls, we made the musical swirls for which these instruments are so famous. On the second evening we caught up on our interrupted honeymoon in the temple built as a monument to love; we were alone, newly married and under the influence of a wonder of the world. The experience elevated hearts and souls to a sweet, recurring memory.

From the Taj Mahal, our next stop was another romantic spot – Udaipur in Rajasthan, home of the Floating Palace and considered one of the most beautiful places in India. We checked into a pleasant hotel with a view of the lake. A short walk revealed the cloud-shrouded floating palace set in the middle of an island. We were, again, among the first post-war tourists moving around town and buying a few treasures. It was, nevertheless, surprising when we had a knock on our door and a representative of the Maharaja of Udaipur invited us to the Floating Palace for drinks and dinner.

Our host made it very clear that though he was politically deposed, he was still a wealthy Maharaja. The food was plentiful and excellent, and to accompany the lavish meal we were served, with a flourish, Fanta! The ubiquitous soft drink of Asia.

After dinner the real fun began. A gigantic photograph book was brought out by the Maharaja himself and he began serious attempts to impress Rebecca by showing her photo after photo of the tigers he had killed. Rebecca, always wearing her emotions on her sleeve, was not the most receptive of audiences. After about the fifteenth tiger the Maharaja finally noticed Rebecca's pained, horrified expression and switched to photos of the former First Lady of the United States, Jacqueline Kennedy, who had been a visitor to the Floating Palace. Mrs. Kennedy toured India during her husband's administration. She was photographed standing for a formal, panoramic portrait with the Maharaja, his brother, the Prince, their wives and the entire palace entourage. What made it so interesting was that Mrs. Kennedy was wearing a traditional Indian sari. As the Maharaja gleefully turned the page, a new view of the beautiful sari into which Mrs. Kennedy had been so tightly wound was revealed. The fabric had actually split in the middle down the back just, according to our host, before the photo was to be taken. The snapshot revealed the Prince grasping the back of The American First Lady's sari and holding it in place so they could get through the photo opportunity.

Our evening as guests of the Maharaja ended quickly when he began to regale us with stories and photos of the record number of crocodiles he had shot on a trip to Africa.

We took our own trip to an Indian wildlife preserve and that turned out to be fantastic. While not a tiger reserve, it was home to many unusual species, but particularly the Giant Siberian Red Cranes that wintered in India. It is thrilling to stroll around a bend in the jungle and spot two of these red, six-foot birds, cavorting in a mud-stomping mating dance.

Next we were off to Varanasi, the old Benares and city of Lord Shiva, located on the Ganges River. Varanasi is one of the holiest places in India. It has been a place of pilgrimage since before recorded history and is the place where all Hindus would like to breathe their last on this plane of existence. This desire was fully demonstrated as our train approached the city. At each stop, more and more corpses of those souls who had not quite made it to the Ganges were being loaded onto the train. As we approached the outskirts of Varanasi, we could see two or three corpses strapped onto the roofs of taxicabs heading towards the city center and the burning ghats on the river.

On our second morning in Varanasi we were awakened by the incredible stench of death wafting into our room from the street. As I craned my neck to peer out the window I discovered what the horrible smell was — a corpse lying below our window. I notified the hotel manager who said he would bring in the "corpse brigade" as quickly as possible to remedy the situation. And in fact, it wasn't too long until a cart with other corpses arrived below our window. We watched the scene, unable to pull ourselves away. The men tried to throw the corpse on top of the pile on an over-loaded cart. There were already so many corpses piled on the cart that ours rolled off – twice. Ah, here now we witness the unique style of Indian problem solving. Ingeniously, a fresh corpse was removed from the cart and left under our window making room for the decaying one that was taken away. A clever solution, it was explained, since the one that was left behind was fresh and wouldn't smell so bad. "Our" corpse found its place on the top of the stack and the cart rumbled off, over the cobblestones, on its way to the burning ghats. Our gawking presence at the window looking down on the drama was acknowledged by the brigade leader with a wave of his hand and a promise for their quick return to collect the new corpse and deliver it to the burning ghats, "this very night" . . . and so they did.

Aside from the strange attraction of the death trade in Vara-nasi, another attraction was that cannabis shops were legal in the city. Plenty of hippies were hanging around, smoking chillums and wandering down to the burning ghats to listen to the skulls pop.

Hindu Varanasi embraces a highly spiritual Buddhist corner. We visited Sarnath, home of Deer Park where the Dharma was first preached by Buddha to five monks. We visited the Sadhu parks and watched the chillums constantly passed among the mendicants. Rickshaw was the only form of transportation available. A quarter of a million drivers had official operator's licenses. Our driver guided us to shops offering masala chai, tasty curries and cool, refreshing lassis, the traditional yogurt drink made more interesting by the addition of an edible form of cannabis and known as bhang – one sip was much too foreign to our western taste buds.

I began hiring a boat, daily, and we were rowed across the mile-wide Ganges. We'd stop and I'd take a brief swim in the middle of the river where the water was clear and green. After crossing we would have a picnic on the remarkably barren shore considering the overpopulated crowded city on the opposite side. As we ate and relaxed it was with great pleasure that we listened to the resonant gongs, lilting bells and hypnotic chants drifting across the holy waters from a multitude of spiritual temples. Our simple, inexpensive pleasure came to an abrupt halt when I swam into a corpse.

Chapter Four

"We have found these clothes, this time and place, this personality.
If we go toward the light and praise others,
it comes pouring back."

RUMI

CALIFORNIA, SUMMER OF 1971

My journey with Rebecca to Asia started with a reconnection to a musician I'd gotten to know in Chicago. Jelly Roll Troy was a bass player who had been on the road making a living as a musician since he was 14 years old. Jelly Roll played with a teenage sensation, one-hit-wonder group called the Kallaen Twins. The handsome brothers, riding their good looks and radio airplay, appeared on "Dick Clark's Cavalcade of Stars Tours" with Chuck Berry, Johnny Rivers and the Rhonettes. Now in his early twenties, Jelly Roll had relocated to the San Francisco Bay Area to be part of Mike Bloomfield's blues band. Bloomfield was creating his solo band in the wake of his artistic fame with Bob Dylan and the Paul Butterfield Blues Band.

I caught up with Jelly on his way to jam with Jerry Garcia and Howard Wales at the Matrix Club one Monday night in San Francisco. The set was loosey-goosey but innovative and accomplished. Roger Troy, his birth name, sang a namesake blues cover, "Jelly Jelly," in a powerful yet angelic gospel-flavored, white blues voice. He used his voice as an instrument displaying the broad range the blues needs to be emotionally flavored just right. The song received a standing ovation from the crowded club. Wales was making his musical living as a member of a relocated-from-the-midwest blues band known as A.B. Skhy. They had big money and promotion behind them. Because of that, A.B. Skhy had appeared on a number of desirable big-time gigs. For me it meant backstage passes for the seminal British stars, The Who, at the Fillmore. Unfortunately for A.B. Skhy, they attempted to leave their blues roots for psychedelic experimentation on their first big budget, major label album. It was instantly unsuccessful musically and financially.

Howard Wales was the keyboard player in A.B. Skhy and put together a small budget for a solo album to be the first release by a new label known as Douglas Records. Jelly Roll Troy invited me to check out a session. The other players setting up their instruments when we got there were Curly Cook on guitar, Jerry Garcia from the Grateful Dead on lead guitar and a guy who was introduced to me as Bill Vitt, on drums. All these connections led me to enjoy being on the fringe of what came to be called the "Wales/Garcia" album. I started hanging around, enjoying the artistic process as it unfolded, whenever I could.

The financial underpinnings of the project came from some truly gourmet marijuana that was shipped into the United States in ham tins. When opened, the tins emitted the hiss of a sealed container and out wafted the beautiful bouquet of the colitas inside.

Wales and Garcia were pushing the musical envelope in each session. It was thrilling to hear the collaborative, artistic stretch into electronica, fusion, blues and even Stockhausen. The limited budget, unfortunately, did not allow for a continuous roll of recording tape so many magical and spontaneous moments were lost.

It was also fascinating to hear Jelly Roll's tales from the road, working for a family organization, like the Kallaen Twins were, and have those tales overlapped and intertwined by Garcia's fascinating stories. Garcia had also been on the road at fifteen with a family outfit, some cousins who played bluegrass. Howard Wales, too, was a road veteran and had played behind some Motown acts. Howard had also played a memorable organ part on what was the Dead's signature tune, "Truckin'." Wales added his off-beat and acerbic wit to the road stories.

The deal and musical direction were Wales' idea and Garcia praised him, on more than one occasion, for his tones and abilities. In turn, Wales would chide Garcia about the quality of his sidemen and mock the Grateful Dead's occasionally out-of-tune musical renditions. A number of times I heard him pointedly wonder if the Dead's rhythm guitarist, Bobby Weir, could perform anything other than "chinca, chinca." The concept of the album was loose and free-form with a lot of tokin', jokin' and frequent-food-breaks kind of musical fun for the engineers, roadies and happy fringe few.

One afternoon, the art for their album cover, created by Abdul Mati, was brought to the studio. Abdul Mati had done a dramatic LP cover for the Eric Clapton/Stevie Winwood English super group called Blind Faith featuring a naked, young girl holding a model airplane. Mati had created a naked young girl, holding nothing, for the Wales/Garcia album.

Everybody in attendance wondered aloud if the representation was too young, as the model for the art work appeared to be, as Wales said, "Only about twelve years old."

Garcia liked the artistic effort if not the concept or the subject.

The road-hardened and Americana expert, Jelly Roll said, "In the southern U.S. they call that young stuff . . . 'hooter roll.' Which led to a recording-free afternoon of tales, jokes and tokes.

"Hooteroll" stuck as the album's title.

The first desire of all musical groups is a problem-free sound system and dependable transportation. Rabid Rakow was so-called because of his ultra-wired high energy and his big deal-a-minute business propositions. He constantly worked on both and snapped photos of the musicians in between the proposals.

Rakow's main, grand scheme was to have the Grateful Dead own a corporate-style fleet of cars. The plan was to have one car for each player, manager and the sound crew. Rakow found a used car lot full of old Hertz rental cars and bought six. Five were for the Dead and one was for himself for putting the deal together. My old friend, Big Red Ted saved me from being "volunteered" to drive one of the junkers off the lot. As I was, leaving Garcia gave me a patch that read "Keep on Truckin'." As he lit a cigarette from a cigarette, he added, "Get it sewed on something . . . it's somebody's idea . . . to promote the Dead."

It was this unique setting and circumstance that began my love affair with Rebecca. Big Red Ted took me out of the musical funfest and led me towards that fantastic relationship.

Ted showed up at the studio with excitedly offered apologies and dragged me out of the session. On the way to the parking lot he told me that a Tibetan Lama had been smuggled into the U.S. from Canada and was hiding from the powers that be, including Nixon and Henry Kissinger. The State Department had an all-points bulletin out on the Lama just to appease the Communist Chinese. Ted said Nixon was going to play the "China Card" to get re-elected and Kissinger was going to make a big deal about deporting this Lama back to occupied Tibet as a diplomatic symbol of potential political cooperation between the two nations. I felt obliged to help my persuasive, concerned friend help this Lama.

My knowledge of Tibetan history, religion and politics was limited. I had read one chapter on Buddhism while taking a course on comparative religions when I went to college. Tibet I could find on a map. Ted said I would get a rush course and the Cliff Notes version on the way to a suitable hiding place.

"He's a master of books and is bringing the ancient wisdom and knowledge of Tibet here in order to share it with the world," said Ted. "You love to read and write," he added. "It's the perfect initiation for you."

The Lama was known as Tarthang Tulku. He could speak English fairly well, having spent a period of his life as a refugee monk in Alexandria, Egypt. He chose Alexandria because of its infamy in human history for having its libraries burned. The Lama was hopeful the world would not allow it to happen again.

Big Ted suggested the Sierra Nevada Mountains, being similar to the geography of Tibet, might ease the fugitive Lama's mind. It was summertime and fairly easy to secure a ski cabin in the Lake Tahoe area. Being off-season, the ski chalet only had a small TV, AM radio and paper plates. I explained sit-com TV and the rules of baseball. In halting English he explained the Path and how he meditated to physically change the brain for positive happiness; how to "center" oneself. By the fourth baseball game Tarthang Tulku was more than impressed by the variety of skills neces- sary to be a baseball player . . . throwing, hitting and especially a player running down a long fly ball.

During the next week, while attending to the Lama, I received a simple education in practical Buddhism from this incredible man who had traveled many a hard mile. He gave me unusual perspectives on life by debating intellectual thought. Tibetans are great debaters and much of their learning is tested in high pow- ered and energetic debates. The Lama posed problems and spoke philosophically and in metaphors. His teachings would begin with a statement – such as, "you must go into the Tibetan mind, the mind that believed in times past that thunder comes from the roar of a dragon, to consider what I am now going to tell you." He taught me the Tibetan style of theological and philosophical debate wherein points are emphasized by slapping one's palm with the back of one's other hand. This ritualistic part of the debate, he informed me, keeps the debate from getting too emotional and from being reduced to rigid argument rather than a fluid exchange of thought.

I was able to work in a good hike and swim every day in Lake Tahoe while the Lama did his meditations. After about ten days, Ted returned and told me he had made other living arrangements. An underground accommodation for Lama Tarthang Tulku seemed safe in Berkeley. Former Peace Corps volunteers had offered refuge.

Tarthang Tulku told us that, before we left for Berkeley, he must perform a blessing and water ceremony for Lake Tahoe. Ted explained that lakes were considered very sacred in Tibet, so to him it came as no surprise. I saw it as a last chance to be on a beautiful lake and suggested that we rent a boat and water ski out. I celebrated the end of my days of unexpected, enforced, though not unpleasant, spiritual training by skiing to where the Lama would perform his ceremony. Ted skied back.

The vision of me and Ted in bathing suits with the Lama in traditional saffron and burgundy robes was, no doubt, unusual when the rented speed boat returned to the marina.

A girl handled the paperwork for the rented boat dockside. The way the sun caught her golden tresses and healthy glow, she looked angelic. Her reaction to the burgundy and gold robed gentleman, carefully off-loading an ornate prayer box, was as if a Tibetan Lama arrived every hour or so. As Ted settled the bill, I officially ended my monkish period by throwing a couple of my best lines out. The lovely lass threw back a general invitation to a party that night with some of her college friends who were doing the "summer job in Tahoe thing."

Rebecca and I were inseparable, although sometimes only in spirit, from that night on. She gave her employer two weeks notice and joined me in the Bay Area. Early in our relationship together, a bit of a hint of a previous romantic crush began to leak into our conversations. Though she had never met him, it seemed (to my ever more acute ears) that she had an infatuation with Bob Weir of the Grateful Dead. I knew a way to stomp any further thoughts of him out of my new love's head. I wrangled an invitation into one of the last of the Wales/Garcia sessions and said I was going to bring a big fan. My plan was, at some point, to throw a few leading lines to Howard Wales that would set up one of his bitter, twisted remarks, hopefully, about Bobby Weir . . . "chinca, chinca."

When we got to the studio, however, it was not the first, nor the last time, that I would see a musical collaboration that had changed totally and completely. Being in Tahoe and focused on the teachings of the lama, I hadn't known that Jelly Roll Troy had been in a coma as a result of a gastro-intestinal attack. Though Jelly had recovered, there were near-death consequences. Jerry Garcia had brought John Kahn in to replace him on bass. Garcia had quite obviously taken over leadership and direction of not only the musicians but the recording sessions. He was pushing hard for completion of the new album. There were no Bobby Weir "chinca, chinca" jokes from Howard, so I foolishly and childishly blurted Weir's name, caught myself and shut up as the session ended. Garcia casually replied that they always put Weir in the front-middle of the Grateful Dead promotion photos because "Bobby is the best looking guy in the band."

Chapter Five

*"There is a Bazaar where everyone seems to be buying and selling
things from all over the world, and you meet all kinds
of people. It is as noisy as hell and very dirty but a very
nice and interesting place in a lovely valley."*
A CHINESE TRAVELER, 700 AD

ASIA, 1972

After the unrelenting difficulty of travel across India, part
of which included the specter of war, Kathmandu exuded
a feeling of welcome. Our friends, Bill and Patty and Ted and
Cathy, were already there as previously agreed. We checked into
the Snow Lion Hotel, famous for being the headquarters of Sir
Edmund Hillary at the time he undertook his first successful as-
cent of Mt. Everest with the Sherpa, Tenzing Norgay. Other hotels

2nd floor cannabis store

Cathy Worcester

had their own history and attributes. The black market money exchange was in the Panorama. Hash and ganja came by room service at the Inn Eden.

I began searching for horses to pro-vide local transport and we moved into a house known as the Double Dorje in Bodha. Horseback riding offered not only a pleasurable means to take in the remarkable scenery; it also served well during our forays to and from the commercial center.

Bodha is one of the more isolated corners of the Kathmandu Valley where Bill, Patty, Ted and Cathy had taken up residence. It was about eight miles from the city center of Kathmandu. Bodha is home to a giant stupa built at the time of the Buddha's death and one of the eight most revered spots in the Buddhist world.

The giant eyes on top of the great stupa structure lend a cer-tain beneficence to the surrounding area. Shops selling chai and chaat, prayer flags, singing bowls and cymbals encircled the stu-pa. Pilgrims to the holy site ritually circumambulated the shrine.

Life was very simple and very primitive. It was necessary to take appropriate precautions to stay healthy. Going to market, carefully shopping and cooking, boiling water, and house keeping were necessary activities and yet there was still plenty of time for enjoying meals with friends and exploring the exotic culture. The whole valley ran out of food about eight at night and provisions would not be available until the trucks arrived with produce the next morning.

Bill and I purchased Russian-made motorcycles. There was practically no traffic, dirt roads were the norm and I cannot remember even one traffic light.

One day, the Hog Farm bus, with Wavy Gravy as its admiral, limped into Kathmandu, infusing the scene with a whiz-bang but weary energy. The grueling trip up the steep mountain road was not achieved without difficulty. Nepalese bus drivers enjoy pointing out to the Western tourists the unreachable remains of all types of vehicles that didn't make it across, including other buses with less astute drivers. Unfortunately, Wavy and his wife, Billy Jean, would soon have to leave for a U.S. hospital due to Wavy's bad back. One of the Hog Farmers was Dr. Larry Brilliant – a genuine M.D. and counter-culture hero, and he insisted Wavy go home.

Dr. Larry Brilliant and his wife with the Hog Farm bus

German Ted, Torry Wells & their child Guava

Soon after the Hog Farmers arrived, a Mercedes-Benz van, driven by a guy known as German Ted, pulled into the stupa area. He and his wife, Tory, had with them the first Afghan mastiff dog that I had ever seen, an incredibly fantastic specimen of the canine world. I approached Ted and found out that he had acquired the dog in Afghanistan where the breed was rare and had, for centuries, been guard dogs for the caravans. I determined then that I would, someday, have one of those proud, majestic beasts.

It was at this time in Kathmandu that we all became aware of the plight of the Tibetans. Thousands of Tibetan refugees were fleeing to Nepal from the Communist Chinese takeover of their country. They were living in mud and squalor in tents all across the Kathmandu Valley. They nevertheless seemed to us to be very bright, happy, energetic people, exuding sheer goodwill, despite their hardship. They drew all of us into their lives and we found ourselves wanting to help them.

But first, I began a quest to find some hash to potentially smuggle to Amsterdam. Since it was legal, I had very few problems obtaining it; but the Nepalese were quite adept at controlling its leaving their country. Nonetheless, in my explorations, I established some valuable connections with customs officials and other government appointees who would prove beneficial in the future in other ways that had nothing to do with hashish smuggling.

Our home, the Double Dorge, was a sprawling 150-year-old structure that, like all houses in the valley, had ceilings that were less than six feet tall. Hog Farm bus rider, Milan Melvin, shared half the house with us. Milan had a long, checkered history on the scene. He was one of the first underground disc jockeys to play rock and roll music on FM radio in San Francisco in the late '60s. One night, on the air, he made the startling announcement that he had been an FBI informant infiltrating anti-war activists. After a personal 180, Melvin married the sister of Joan Baez – Mimi Farina. While the marriage was short-lived, it did give Milan an odd credence that weighed against his former informant career.

Our next-door neighbor was an attractive Canadian woman dubbed "Buddy Lynn" for her easy manner with males. She introduced me to General Wangdoo. The General was one of the heads of the Khampa resistance – guerillas who were fighting on behalf of Tibet and funded by the CIA. They were located in the Mustang Province at the outermost reaches of the Nepalese/Tibet border. I spent afternoons at Buddy Lynn's Bodha house, fascinated and intrigued by Wangdoo's tales of life and the battles that he had fought, which were less militarily significant and more a thorn in the side of the Chinese Communists. His story began with the CIA "recruiting" eight teenage Tibetan boys to train them for high altitude mountain work. In 1959, the freshly trained teens were parachuted back into Tibet with radios strapped on their backs for the purpose of starting the first resistance cells. According to General Wangdoo, he was the only one of the eight who actually survived that first drop. Also, it became apparent in his tales that he was a CIA favorite because he grasped that they desired paper more than body count. His guerilla outfit would raid storage depots and remote Chi-Com military outposts and General Wangdoo would come out with information, such as how many gallons of diesel fuel were being used to supply the convoys that brought the Chinese military up into Lhasa and other parts of Tibet. The CIA spooks were much more desirous of this kind of information and numbers to sift. The guerilla attacks were mostly on the re-supply convoys.

Buddy Lynn eventually turned Wangdoo on to LSD and cocaine and bragged about having sex with him. It was also the General's great pleasure to hear any music by Jimi Hendrix. Another twist in the story was the General's appearance. While at training school in Colorado, he was shown many John Wayne and American Old West, cowboy and Indian movies for entertainment at night. And as fashion sense and style would have it, the General, not speaking any English at the time or understanding any of the dialogue of the cowboy movie plots, adopted the style of John Wayne's adversaries, i.e., the Mexicans. He wore pants with conchos down the sides and bandoliers of bullets slung across his chest, a Tibetan Pancho Villa in fine attire.

Rebecca and I made our initial attempts at trekking in Nepal by going up to Nagarkot, the first high ground out of the valley where one could have a clear view of the majesty of Mount Everest. Going through the remote mountain villages and coming upon a festival with big horns, colorful masks, and dancers dressed as animal spirits was truly exciting and fueled the fires for more adventuresome treks.

When we returned from Nagarkot, we were invited to the wedding of Hog Farmer Tom Glen and his gorgeous Tibetan girlfriend, Latchu. Then, as the prayer wheel turns, things got really unbelievable.

Buddy Lynn married General Wangdoo. She whispered to me after the vows that she would set it up so that I could accompany them to the Mustang area where the guerilla army was headquartered. The only Tibetan fighters I'd seen were the ones that hung around Lynn's Bodha home. They would come and go at the

General's bidding with fistfuls of one-hundred dollar bills supplied by the CIA. The General told me that a one-hundred-dollar bill, in Mustang, bought one pound of rice. Like the value of the money, "everything" he said, "was totally out of control." To his dismay, audio cassette players with big speakers had been rolled into the guerilla camps and a speech by the Dalai Lama was broadcast calling for a peaceful resolution and an end to the attacks on the Communist Chinese.

Three days after their marriage, Buddy Lynn was attempting to continue behaving like a Western woman in a typical Western marriage. The way that General Wangdoo's wife should be conducting her life was totally different. The General thought that Lynn's wifely duties consisted of cleaning, cooking and doing the laundry. No more Western visitors and no more intellectual and historical discussions were permitted with their neighbors. He expressed this by grabbing Lynn behind the neck and frog-marching her out of our Double Dorge house right in front of us in order to make his point. It was the last time we saw the General. Within weeks he and his main mobile attack force were ambushed and killed in a high mountain pass by Nepalese army sharpshooters.

Chapter Six

"In Italy, for thirty years under the Borgias, they had warfare, terror, murder and bloodshed but they produced Michelangelo, Leonardo DaVinci and the Renaissance. In Switzerland they had brotherly love and they had 500 years of democracy and peace; and what did that produce? The coo-coo clock!"

HARRY LIME, *"THE THIRD MAN"* BY GRAHAM GREENE

Dutch Bob tried to recruit anyone of worth he met in the Kathmandu Valley to assist him in his Hash-to-Amsterdam deals.

"I come from a small country that must hold back the sea to exist. We have been forced to go far from our loving homes and deal in spices to survive," was his sales pitch. "Tea, saffron, cinnamon, hashish or coffee . . . any and all spices," he added, like a snake oil salesman, mumbling and choking on "hashish" every time he pitched it.

"Amsterdam and Holland will lead the citizens of the planet from old laws and prisons to freedom and legalization. Help us!" Dutch Bob pleaded, adding "Nepalese diplomats have had a long, successful hash smuggling history. Nepal, like my beloved Holland, is a small, desperate country, thus entrepreneurial."

Dutch Bob eventually convinced me that it was necessary for me to help him with hashish deliveries to his homeland via diplomatic courier. Although I was opposed to the idea of dealing with diplomats because of the potential betrayal from that kind of intrigue, I went along. I needed money. He insisted that if the hash clubs in Amsterdam were not supplied with the product, they would not be able to stay in business. And from the first two clubs, there were now nearly ten . . . strength in numbers was the idea.

Rebecca stayed with our friends and I headed off to Amsterdam in my white linen suit; my image of choice as an international business man. I had noticed that a white suit drew respect from immigration officers, customs agents and airline personnel.

My role in this deal was to ship the trunk and pick up the money. Dutch Bob monitored the actual transporting of the soft Nepalese 'tolas' as the fingers of hash were known. The sheer high quality of this non-export, specialty hash – so very, very rare, was part of the reason I acquiesced.

Bob had instructed me to go to the National Olympic Stadium when I arrived in Amsterdam and take a sauna on Tuesday afternoon, the day that the stadium was free and open to the public. Someone would give me a red tie to wear and then the money. I made my way there and found, however, that the facilities had been taken over by the Dutch police who maintained control of "open day" by giving the evil-eye and the cold-shoulder treatment to any and all. I enjoyed the sauna, took the cold plunge and ignored the vacant stares of the police. No one contacted me, no red tie – nothing but an unsettling experience.

I went back to the hotel and telegraphed Bob that I had a wonderful bath and nothing more. He telegraphed back to me that I should return on Thursday. There would be a pass at the door. The pass was waiting for me and I went into the locker room and undressed. My first thought was that the man approaching me was a locker room attendant. He tossed me a gym bag and said "On your way, druggie, don't use this place! What are you doing here, are you some kind of American hippie?" Then he left. Inside the bag was a red tie.

I got dressed, put on the red tie and headed out of the Olympic Stadium. As soon as I got outside the door, I noticed that the same fake locker room attendant was waiting. He said, "May I offer you a ride back into town?" When I got into the back seat of the car, there sat the Nepalese diplomat. We rode into Amsterdam and other than "very nice tie," little was said. I was given an ornate box that was filled with Dutch guilders, "for local expenses." I telegraphed Bob that the first part of the arrangement had been completed and he directed me, by return wire, to a travel agent where there would be a plane ticket waiting for me that led to my share of the profits.

The destination on the plane ticket was Saigon, Vietnam. One would imagine that Saigon, in the middle of the Vietnam War, would not be the first choice for a business meeting, but in fact, anybody could come and go, at their own risk. Except for the tension one felt in human interactions, most of the sprawling city showed no signs of war.

I met Dutch Bob and two other Hollanders at The Continental, an old French-colonial hotel. I was somewhat stunned at the way my share of the profits was remitted. Proudly the Hollanders showed me that they had managed to obtain some "ice cold" Heineken beers and proceeded to pay me in gold which, they said, was "better than money."

At the time of this transaction, the Vietnamese had been at war for about 30 years, first against the colonial French occupation and now the United States. This period of conflux had long established an economy based on gold. Not only were the pieces of gold precise in weight, but they were molded into a curved shape so that they would fit the contours of the human body and slide into thin leather belts for transport.

Bob elicited a toast and agreement from his Dutch buddies and me that "we are well on our way to saving world travelers, pilgrims and freedom lovers from tyranny!"

Then he weighed the profits.

I flew out of Saigon with gold strapped all over my body. When I got to Hong Kong, I quickly detached myself from the situation and sold the gold for about 80 cents on the dollar. I missed my sweetheart and always worried about her waiting in a wild corner of the world. Giving up a few points of profit was stacked against each priceless hour in her arms back in Kathmandu.

Chapter Seven

"Hanoi Hannah – averaged about a man a day –
when she wasn't working –
she kept the coffee perkin'
for a guy that didn't have to pay."
"HANOI HANNAH," R. MCGUINN AND J. LEVY

Due to international airspace restrictions during the "cease-fire," as it was called, between India and Pakistan, there were no flights out of Asia into Afghanistan from anywhere except Bangkok. So, from Kathmandu, Rebecca and I flew to Thailand.

Downtown Bangkok, in 1971, consisted of small, one-man noodle stands scattered at random and mixed among a dozen buildings that had full-on Western style boutiques, escalators and air conditioning. Gucci was the most popular boutique. The American Express office, where all nationalities received mail, was located high up in one of those skyscrapers. The panoramic view it presented revealed a modern, suburban, American-like development surrounding Bangok, that was being furiously constructed from money fueled by the Vietnam War. South Africans, Italians and the French were making nice profits off that war, as were Americans from every state. All were cashing checks, buying traveler's checks or wiring funds back home. News and gossip flowed as fast as the indexing of international currencies.

Bangkok was mainly a pass-through plane hub on the way to somewhere else. There were two or three hotels that accommodated the pilots and airline personnel as well as most of the passengers who were just transiting through on their way to other destinations. One notorious hotel was The Malaysia. It was infamous for its junkie clientele and Thai hangers on. Another hotel featured great ganja connections.

We chose to stay for a couple of nights at the hotel known for its weed connection to get our hands on some herb. Once that was accomplished we moved to the classy Oriental Hotel, which was an inexpensive four-star wonder. The Oriental had four bungalows built as high-end suites in the early 1900s. Rattan ceiling fans, bamboo shutters, a king-sized bed, mosquito nets and night ginger wafting in on a Chao Phraya River breeze are undeniably aphrodisiacs.

The opposite of loving sex was a constant presence, however. Rebecca had her first encounter with the infamous Asian escort girls. Almost every male we met had on his arm a lovely bar girl. At this time, most of these girls were from the starving tribal highlands where their families were forced to sell their daughters to Cholon Chinese agents. The "agents" encouraged the girls into the local sex profession if they were pretty. The less fortunate were shuffled off to Arab seaport brothels. In Thailand, the girls were given a few days of training and then sent out to work under controlled circumstances in the bars. They could speak little, if any, English. Rebecca interacted with them politely. They were very well mannered.

One girl would generally stay with the man who paid her "bar fee" for as long as he was in the country. It wasn't unusual to see two or three such escort girls at dinner or any social situation.

All of the nightlife took place in the infamous Patpong Road area. This two-block wide and six-block long strip had clubs with names such as "Mississippi Queen," "Chicago Gangsters" and "Super Star." The strip was an electronic-neon excess gone wild. Video screens and computer light shows were found here and recorded rock and roll blared out of the clubs. American soldiers on R&R mixed it up with Danish engineers, Middle Eastern merchants, Japanese electronic experts, and international travelers

like us. The males sported sweet young things on their arms. Anyone could get a small bag of second-rate ganja from the circling
cab drivers. Barkers hawked clubs with weird sex shows . . . "see a
pussy smoke a cigarette" . . . or promising an up-close view of girls
shooting ping pong balls out of their vaginas. "Hey Joe . . . inside
you gonna see a pussy drink Coca-Cola and then you drink the
Coca-Cola . . . !" A herd of staggering sailors eagerly paid money
for the privilege.

The restaurants offered an astounding array of culinary delights derived from the European countries of their "war rich"
clients. There was a German hofbrau, a French bistro, a Swed-
ish smorgasbord and an American cheeseburger shack. Rebecca
and I absorbed the scene but after an hour's worth of loud Rolling Stones and Otis Redding, and a wonderful meal at one of
the many ethnic restaurants strung around the area, we'd had
enough.

The following morning we took an escorted tour through the
museum, the King's palace grounds and a major Buddhist temple
that was home to a five-ton gold statue. It was a rich historical and
cultural experience, the exact opposite of the previous evening. We
barely had time to digest the magnificent artisanship of Thailand
past or the exotic architecture of the royal enclave before we were
notified that we had a four-hour window of opportunity to get on
a plane to Kabul.

Chapter Eight

Afghan: unruly or untamed.
Afghanistan: land of the unruly.

The house we were lucky enough to find was actually an estate consisting of four acres enclosed within a 24-foot high, 3-foot thick mud wall. A nephew of the King had been sent to Oxford University in England in the 1950s and built it after he returned to Afghanistan when he realized the value of good water. He located the estate where the Kabul River flowed out of the mountains. The home was English Tudor style with two bathrooms that had Japanese bathtubs and regular European-style flush toilets, a welcome amenity in 1970s Afghanistan. On the grounds was a stable area with quarters for a groom as well as a combination gateman and guard's house. We enjoyed a beautiful garden and grape arbor and there was an area for children to play that had a jungle gym, slide and sandbox. The children of our Western guests were always delighted by the familiarity. The owner was the great-grandson of the original builder and was the current Deputy Prime Minister of Afghanistan. Our oasis was located on the far edge of Kabul proper, half a kilometer from an edifice that was built to honor the defeat of Alexander the Great by the Afghan people – Jangalak – the battle of 100,000. "Lak" is the Farsi word for 100,000.

Our good fortune continued. The landlord recommended a

business known as "The 24 Hour Service" that catered to diplomats stationed in Kabul. Whatever was needed, this service promised to provide it within 24 hours.

I followed our landlord's instructions to Diplomat Row in Kabul in an attempt to find a cook and other staff to run our estate. The 24 Hour Service recommended a chef named Abdul who had worked at the Intercontinental Hotel. He was fired because he was caught smoking hashish. I scooped him up and brought him out to the house to have him prepare an "audition" dinner and then hired him on the spot. He quickly became one of the most valuable cogs in the wheel of our daily life, contributing to our healthy, happy existence. He was very well trained in German, French and traditional Afghan cuisine. Rebecca taught him how to cook Mexican food.

Also, I met two teenage boys who had done the overland ordeal to Kabul: Mark Krause and Archie Gardner had hit the road within weeks of high school graduation. They introduced me to the Afghans, Sakhi and Ghiaz.

Ghiaz's story was that he took the train to Iran with as much hash as he could carry. He jumped off the moving caboose into the boarder area no-mans land and walked the *herb dangerous* into a small village where it was transferred to his European employers. Iranian law meted out a sentence of death by torture for Afghans caught smuggling anything. To Ghiaz, by comparison, the opposite direction through the Khyber Pass was a "walk in the park."

Sakhi grew up in Balkh. For centuries Balkh was home to the world's best hash-pollen farmers and hand pressers. Sakhi took Mark and me

Ghiaz and his horse Sultan

Mark Krause and Sahki in Balkh

north to show us what he had access to. He carried an old flintlock rifle for protection everywhere we went.

Afghanistan's national game of *buzkashi* is well-known around the world and is played with the carcass of a headless, hoofless calf or goat. It is a rough and violent version of polo that tests the skills of man and horse. I set out to find a *buzkashi* horse to ride. I found a beautiful white stallion and, against the Afghani tradition of naming a horse after its color, I named this one "Sazz" – or music – for his tremendous, strong yet smooth gait. He was perfectly trained. Sazz, only recently retired from the game, became a beloved member of our family. I sometimes thought he missed the games. Sazz certainly loved to run.

The gardener also served as the resident caretaker of the estate and he was happy to continue his role when we rented the house. He lived on the estate and maintained it for the Deputy Prime Minister, who used it primarily for his daughters to romp and play behind the walls in the children's playground. In an Afghan tradition, I also hired Rustan, a eunuch, to perform the role of a traditional housekeeper and cleaner.

I was able to find a small well-trained, Bamiyan breed of horse we named Red Flame for Rebecca to ride. This led to our first big cultural problem. Women were strictly forbidden from riding horses. On our first horseback ride, we were greeted by a hail of rocks at Karta-i-sah, the first village beyond our home.

After directing Rebecca to head for home and fueled by righteous indignation, as I'd never felt before, I stormed through the village market, kicking over fruit and vegetable stands, pulling down tent awnings and slashing at any and all with my *buzkashi* whip before galloping towards home after her.

Our next ride through Karta-i-sah village was without incident. However, at Kartasang, the last village before the Kabul River dropped from the mountains, we had another screaming, pelting attack. This frenzied mob even included some women. Rebecca raced off and my response was careful and quick . . . a surprise taste of village square destruction for Kartasang.

This couldn't go on, of course, without escalating so I implored my landlord, the Deputy Prime Minister, to hold a *jirga*, or council, with the headman of each village and explain that my wife was a Western girl and we would be riding through their villages. We would not tolerate being stoned. Both headmen eventually agreed to the Deputy Prime Minister's superior political pressure; however, we all had to go to each village and conduct a charade where the headmen fervently waved their arms and shouted it was forbidden. The Deputy Prime Minister explained to me, on the way home, that without this theatrical show each man would have signed his own trip to a beheading or the stoning stake.

Chapter Nine

"No great genius was ever without some tincture of madness."
ARISTOTLE

R ebecca and I were invited to visit Lahore by a freaky group of actors who came through Kabul and charmed their way into staying a few days in Jangalak. They had talent, wit and wild looks. The theatrical troupe was a counter-culture sensation in Italy and had just appeared in the Fellini film "Roma." Their fame stemmed from a brilliant scene in a previous Felleni blockbuster cinema hit. These "artistes" ended up in Lahore by signing a three-movie deal portraying drug-dealing hippies in Pakistani films.

Members of the theatrical troupe in our garden

Lahore was actually quite cosmopolitan. There was a thriving gay scene that was totally open and tolerated. We spent about five days there at a wonderful house with beautiful hanging gardens. Hashish was openly smoked in a few places where modern rhythm-oriented Pakistani music was played. Though rare, there were two or three very privileged women in attendance. This was the perk of being a female star in Pakistani films – you could go out in public in the company of foreigners and listen to music. After a while, I left Rebecca in the safety of the film colony and went up to meet Montreal Michael in Islamabad.

Pakistan is an artificially created country where five distinctly different tribes were cobbled together under one flag. Islamabad was the artificially created capitol. The only unifier was the Muslim religion. A difficult political situation was created because the tribes spoke five different languages.

The Grand Peace Mosque dominated the city that was created in the fifties and modeled after Western communities. All the houses had a driveway to the garage, a big front yard, and rambling, ranch-style homes with eight-foot high picture windows in front. Carefree, American TV sit-com families lived in neighborhoods and houses not unlike these built in the new Pakistani capital city. What made it so surreal was that instead of enclosing that big front yard with a picket fence or shrub border, the California-ranch-style homes were surrounded by high razor-wire fences. All the big picture windows were covered with massive anti-theft grills and the garages were boarded over and permanently closed.

Zulfiqar Ali Bhutto was the very progressive Prime Minister who was running things in Pakistan. Bhutto had graduated with honors from the University of California in 1950 and was admitted to Oxford. He embraced the American Federalist system and professed a dream of melding the five distinct tribal areas into one modern state. Many first-generation Pakistani leaders were heavily influenced by having been educated in the U.S. of the 1950s.

California ranch-style homes in safe neighborhoods were their vision. The razor-wire fences were the reality.

Prime Minister Bhutto made a fatal flaw in his political maneuvering. There was a great jockeying for what the official language of the new Pakistan would be. All these years after the creation of the country, the actual lingua franca of Pakistan was Urdu. Urdu was a coarse and profane multi-ethnic language that had developed out of the military in the nineteenth century. Bhutto preferred Sind. Sind was a beautiful old language that was still spoken in only one part of Pakistan by the intelligensia and wealthiest class. Choosing Sind to be the national language was a grave political miscalculation on Bhutto's part. Bhutto went from being the darling of a military establishment that had fought India to a stalemate in the 1971 war, to facing trumped-up charges that sent him to the gallows.

The poetic Sind language brought to mind Pakistani art and culture and was spoken by the cinema community in Lahore. Urdu symbolized Islamabad's garage doors nailed shut and dry swimming pools and was the metaphor for a backwards march toward religious fundamentalism.

Montreal Michael had been in Islamabad for six months and was slowly but surely assembling the components from the city's scientific supply outlets necessary to distill pollen and create hash oil. It was a tedious and unpleasant task but he was undaunted and determined to see his hash oil dream factory built.

Michael met two other Canadians in Islamabad buying laboratory equipment at a scientific supply outlet for the same purpose. Cadillac and the Mad Professor were from British Columbia and, sharing the same nationality and the same purpose, they all became associates. We all went out for kabobs and info exchange.

We talked it through, always admiring the great, though somewhat bizarre, entrepreneurial skills of anyone who could come up with an idea like this. The Mad Professor, in a kindly manner, explained that Montreal Michael, while a genius, would never be able to build the elaborate factory that he was contemplating. He said that the seals that were needed to secure the lab pipe-works were not made well enough in Asia, and thus were dangerously unreliable. They would not be able to handle the engineering tasks that Michael was designing. The Mad Professor suggested a smaller, slower version that produced an ounce of hash oil a day, instead of a gallon an hour. The Cadillac offered to share the blueprints.

Seriously pondering their suggestions, I went back to Lahore to get Rebecca and return to Kabul. I was very glad to be rockin' in my sweet baby's arms again. Unfortunately the rockin' didn't last long because I was called back to Karachi, Pakistan, by an excited Dutch Bob.

Chapter Ten

"If you have a job without aggravation, you don't have a job."
MALCOLM FORBES

Dutch Bob made "arrangements" through some Dutch Embassy fringe employees to pay off Karachi customs officials. Every three or four months I would put the overland-out-of-Kabul-to-Karachi trip together. Dutch Bob took it airport-to-airport into Europe after that. Then I would break away from our idyllic life in Jangalak, put on the white linen suit and go to Amsterdam to collect. The demand for Tibetan carpets and primitive Nepali Tribe jewelry was taking off in Europe as well. Buddha statues were in demand.

Between meetings with Dutch Bob I found time to fly back to the States to visit my friend Bill Wassman. Bill had purchased the top floor of an old warehouse in New York City's SoHo district. It was a 4400 sq. ft., well-lit skeleton. He had a double bed, a coffee pot and a refrigerator. I brought in a futon, blanket and pillow as a house warming present. An actor named Robert DeNiro bought the floor below to fix up for his mother, Bill said.

Bill and I went out to Max's Kansas City club to hear Lou Reed with his new band, but we couldn't get into the place. Outside in the crowd, also unsuccessful in gaining entrance, was a tall, good looking blond man about our age who was wearing a baseball cap from the same university we had attended. It was The Sizzler. We all ended up back at Bill's *l'artiste primitivo* loft and got to know each other over some Durbin poison weed. The Sizzler knew a sailor. The sailor knew somebody who knew somebody on the docks in Brooklyn. Every few months Sizzler visited the sailor in New York City. The Sizzler then drove South African herb 1200 miles to Chicago.

I enlisted Sizz in the Afghan to Amsterdam operation, offering him the position of "cold-hard-cash courier." All the money had to be brought into Afghanistan via money belt and money belt only.

While the money bazaar in Kabul was wide open and you could exchange currencies of any nation in the world for any other, checks of any sort were prohibited.

Anyone associated with an organization that does business based on finding loopholes in various nations' laws generally takes the historical view of it all and the romantic characters involved with the *herbe dangereuse*, as the French call it, must be chivalrous and honorable and streetwise. The Sizzler was just such a guy. The $30,000 to $40,000 cash that would come back to Afghanistan from Amsterdam had to be carried securely on his person. Once he retraced the overland bus route through Iran. Iran was ruled by the ruthless Shah who employed vicious SAVAK underground torture squads. Other times the Sizzler would come directly into Kabul by plane. The Sizz could have, at any time, said that he lost the money by theft, corrupt customs or even legally confiscated. Every penny made it every time.

Also, on the U.S. transit, I reconnected with a couple of old friends from Haight-Ashbury – William VIII and Aggie. William VIII was an accomplished musician who played the bass. He had been the driving force behind organizing us into our failed attempt at a way-too-psychedelic rock and roll band. William VIII and Aggie were inspired to come to Afghanistan and showed up within a month.

Chapter Eleven

"I've been through the desert on a horse with no name
It felt good to be out of the rain
In the desert you can remember your name
'Cause there ain't no one for to give you no pain."
"HORSE WITH NO NAME," AMERICA

When I returned to Afghanistan, German Ted, his wife Tory and their child, Guava, had come back there as well. Remembering his dog in Kathmandu, I immediately enlisted him into helping me search for a mastiff pup and so "Kachook" came into our lives. Kachook was just eight weeks old when I found him after Ted took me up to Bamiyan to locate one of the breed. Where Kachook was actually born is unknown. He was stolen, and had spent the previous two weeks tied to a caravan cart in a walk-for-your-life-or-death situation. The nomads that stole him had sold him to a local Wali the night before German Ted and I arrived. The local Wali had bought him to become a fighting dog, what the Afghans called *sak-jungee*. There were some histrionic Afghan-style negotiations involved. German Ted, invoking local custom, insisted by making the point that it was very, very good luck for the Wali to make a profit so quickly.

When I brought Kachook back to our house, the staff was none too happy about his arrival, even as a charming, playful puppy. These mastiffs were seen as mindless, fierce, attacking beasts.

I saw Kachook's incredible intelligence immediately and he eventually amazed all of our Afghan staff when he quickly learned to obey simple commands. He had four acres to run around in and was a delight from day one. His appearance at my whistle and his obedience to commands had the same effect on our Afghan

household as if a circus tiger had walked in and leaped through a ring of fire. Rebecca and I worked very hard to gentle his nature at every training opportunity.

As spring arrived, I was putting plans together for my dream ride up the old Silk Trail. The Sizzler, who took me at my word and eventually showed up in Afghanistan, and Montreal Michael began gearing up for the ride. I knew we needed a gun for protection so I completed an application to hunt Pamir sheep in the foothills of the Hindu Kush. It cost $2,500 for a license to shoot one of these beasts, which I had no intention of doing, but it allowed me to import a gun for the purpose of hunting and, in our case, protection.

Alejandro, of Goa, also turned up in Afghanistan and was healthy and effervescent. Tory let him borrow her horse and German Ted and I had a ride with him that broke out into a dead run race. Later that night we heard he was arrested during the first known drug squad sweep in Kabul. Tory and Rebecca made immediate contact with the Spanish Embassy and discovered it was true that Alejandro had been caught with 29 grams of golden pollen. There was nothing immediate I could contribute to the situation.

On one of my trips to see Dutch Bob in Amsterdam I purchased an over-and-under rifle – 30-30 on the bottom and a 20-
gauge shotgun on the top.

The planning and preparations for the ride were complete. I
had also, on a previous visit to the States, arranged shipment to
Afghanistan of some much better saddles that were designed for
the U.S. Mounted Park Rangers. These are fine saddles, very light
and practical. The wooden, carpet-covered saddles of Afghanistan
were yet another illustration of how far back in the centuries we
were actually living. The horses were fit and freshly shod as we
rode out – me, Sizz, and Michael with Kachook dogtrotting along.

All along the route, at intervals from four to six hours apart,
we found fortress-like cities that served as rest stops for caravans
along the trade route. We rode into the clay-walled cities of ancient
times where the people lived on one level inside the 30-foot walls
and the earth was dug out in the middle so that the animals lived
in enclosures below the humans. We never knew what would be
available to eat. Food was often only a few chunks of lamb, spinach and rice or millet. Kachook was quite the sensation in each
village where they had, at best, a cur tied up at the fortress gate
to act as sentinel and bark warnings and alert the villagers of
approaching traders or strangers. We reached the Ajanta Pass in
three days.

At the bottom of the Ajanta Pass we met another couple on
horseback who were coming from the opposite direction. They
were Jittendra and Beth and they had undertaken the ride un-
armed and in complete safety, according to them, by being willing
to move slowly and wait to be escorted, family by family and village
to village along the old road. It had taken them thirty days to do
what we did in three. We were all spending a fourth night resting
our horses at the bottom of the pass before heading back to Kabul. Jittendra and Beth's horses needed far more rest before they
could make the hard three days ahead of them. Everything they
were wearing they made themselves. Beth was from Maine, Jit-

tendra from Scotland and together they had been on the road for five years, trading and moving East. They had lived the true traveler's life together, starting out from Jittendra's homeland in Scotland.

It was during our return from Ajanta Pass, about six hours out of Kabul, that I found the stud horse of my breeding dreams. He was a three-year-old Waziri stallion. These wonderful animals have beautifully arched necks and ears that touch each other when raised and were similar to the Tennessee Walker horse. I put down as much money as I could spare and we arranged to meet and buy the stallion in Paghman in a week. The agreed price was the maximum for a good horse – yak lak or 10,000 U.S. dollars.

When we arrived home after the short but intense adventure

Waziri stallion and owner/breeder

I discovered that William VIII and Aggie had showed up, having taken me up on my invitation. They quickly learned some Farsi and William VIII volunteered to take a shipment of hash to Dutch Bob in Karachi. But after successfully shepherding the load across the Khyber Pass, a desolate, violent wasteland, he took his pay and said "once is enough." He was going to study Persian poetry and become accomplished on the oud, an Afghan stringed instrument. "I was scared and stressed so bad" said William VII "I pissed blood by the time I got to Karachi."

On the silk trail

We settled into steadily working on expanding some form of legitimate business. I employed five tailors who turned out Chinese silk brocade harem pants and these garments found a niche through a distributor in Frankfurt. Also, we settled into brainy, solid relationships. Jittendra and Beth joined German Ted, Tory and their growing toddler, Guava, along with William VIII and Aggie, now pregnant, all mixing with a cast of ever-changing, international travelers. Those truly liberated women enjoyed the desert wind in their faces while astride magnificent horses, cantering freely. They held the belief that they were furthering the cause of all women.

Approaching the compound

Children greet us

High walled compound

Inside the coumpund

Chapter Twelve

"When your I.Q. reaches 28 . . . sell!!"
THE COMEDIAN, DR IRWIN COREY, TO A HECKLER

One important thing must be known to understand how pleasant life was in a country most people considered still to be in the Stone Age. The King of Afghanistan owned a huge farm that rivaled the greatest estates of the world. He had outlets in Kabul known as the King's Stores, selling everything from strawberries to succulent lamb and seasonal vegetables – spinach, lettuce, potatoes and legumes. The King's farm fed hundreds of working people, from Diplomat Row to the Royal Family's immediate, highlevel bureaucrats as well as a few health-conscious food-wise international free-style life artists and adventurers.

There was also an outlet that offered wines procured (often stolen) from the French and U.S. Embassies – incredibly great wines and really cheap prices.

Another highlight of life in Kabul was the annual King's *buzkashi* championship game held in the National Stadium, played by the world's greatest horsemen. For a week before the sport, there was a buzz of excited anticipation around the King's Stores where the healthy hipsters mixed with embassy worker bees. The locals all lauded us with eyewitness stories of daring, brilliant feats of horsemanship as well as superior animals performing at their highest level. So it was strange when we did not see anyone around the entrance to the Stadium on the day we attended.

However hardcore, every foreigner living in Kabul was at the Annual Royal Buzkashi match. Rebecca and I were pulled out of the crowd

View from the King's box of the referee explaining the rules as the crowd enters the stadium

and invited by a member of the security guard for the Royal Court to sit in the King's box and view the wild action of that most incredible athletic event. We sat up there with men in suits and ties who joked about it all. The nephew of the King and his cronies were the only ones in the box besides us. We eventually figured out that the beautiful blonde and I were stand-ins for international diplomats who for some reason could not attend. Nevertheless, we enjoyed having the best seats in the house. Afghanistan is heat and dust so the two mounted electric fans in the box were a "royal" touch. The official Royal Photographer took us down to the edge of the arena where the action was. He snapped two black and white photos of the match and promised to have copies made to sell to us. He suggested we use the opportunity to slide into the crowd and

leave before things got even wilder and more supercharged with the fans. "Mumpkin bomb," he cautioned, meaning "maybe a bomb!"

View of the action from the Kings box

After that *buzkashi* match, we met "Billy Batman" and his wife at the anarchy that passed for a taxi stand on the edge of the stadium grounds. They were legendary in Kabul, having survived there since 1969. Billy was older than all of us. It was said he brought hash into New York City in the late 1950s and supplied it to authors and poets, including Alan Ginsberg and William Burroughs as well as jazz greats and stage stars. We enjoyed listening to his tales of the beatnik era. Billy Batman pointed to Hector, the man you see pictured on the cover of white Zig Zag rolling papers, as his role model. Hector's picture was on the Zig Zag wrapper because he was the man who brought hashish to Paris in the 1920s. His hash was enjoyed by the "Lost Generation" of Gertrude Stein, Hemingway, James Joyce and, of course, the hash brownie creator, Alice B. Toklas.

Billy Batman earned the name because of a new technique he created for making hashish. He became interested in me because I had hired a full-time gardener just to tend our cannabis plants and had brought Mexican Gold seeds into Afghanistan. I was conducting my own botanical experiments. I always preferred smoking marijuana to hashish and the only way you could do that in Afghanistan was to grow your own.

Billy had invented what he called "The Batman Technique." He purchased heavy vinyl that was made in Germany and he put hash pollen into the vinyl, wrapped it up and tied it off with tape so that it was about the size of a baseball. He then took a Pakistani shoe mallet and slowly tapped the ball all over, bit by bit. As the heat built up inside the vinyl-covered ball, the pollen liquified. The ball had to be tapped slowly because the vinyl could split and destroy the entire, painstakingly produced product. But if one did it properly, the liquid congealed. When allowed to cool and carefuly unwrapped, the resulting product was the most perfect form of hashish imaginable.

A few days later, when I picked up my photos from the Royal Photographer, any feelings of honor or privilege that I may have

View towards open end of stadium

Royal Afghan Photographer

felt from our selection to view the *buzkashi* match from the Royal Box vanished. The photographer explained that nearly every year someone tried to assassinate the King and his family. Following our departure, a hand grenade was thrown into the Royal Box and, fortunately, did not explode. Three Afghans were killed that day and many more injured, he said . . . trampled to death by the surging, frenzied crowds.

The next morning, I saddled up my horse and took a ride along the river up into the mountains above the Kabul valley. When I returned, Abdul, as usual, had prepared a wonderful breakfast of melon, berries, an omelet and tea served with toasted Afghan bread. Afghan bread was delicious and looked like a giant snowshoe. With butter on it, it tasted like popcorn.

Most days I then headed into the bazaars of Kabul. True treasures from ancient times could be found and many became part of my personal collection and were not for sale.

Kabul had a wide-open money bazaar. There were 95 booths and for a small percentage you could exchange any form of money in the world for any other form of money in the world. The wealthy money-changers enjoyed luncheons at the best restaurants where they were served exquisite kabobs with rice and whatever vegetables were available according to the season. When I had a pocket full of "frogskins" that I was going to trade for Swiss francs, I'd make whoever had the privilege of purchasing the $100 U.S. bills pick up the tab as part of the negotiations. Afterward I'd shop in the old bazaar and then pick up a bouquet of flowers for my sweetie.

Chapter Thirteen

"If you are a Police Dog, where's your badge?"
JAMES THURBER, *1894-1961*

W̶e traveled to every corner of Afghanistan, enjoying amazing Islamic art and archeology from centuries past: the mosque at Mazar i Sharif, the ancient city of Balkh where Alexander married Roxanne and where the tomb of Baba Coo, the smoking saint, is located. It is also the place where Genghis Kahn killed nearly a million people. A little more about Coo: he was the smoking saint of Afghanistan whose name was always invoked by Afghans before smoking hashish, similar to a toast when drinking alcohol. To

Baba Coo's Tomb

Coo, life is always gardens and flowers and life is always spring. Marco Polo references Coo in his journals and admits to enjoying hash with him many times outside the gates of the city of Balkh.

Since it was the season, I drove up to Kundus to see the game of *buzkashi* played up there. Each of the eight Afghan provinces had its own team. Boys who were deemed to be worthy of participating in the game were trained from a very early age. Part of the training was that the boys were struck on the backs of their hands with *buzkashi* whips, one time for each year of their age. This was considered to be necessary preparation for enduring the whips used by the players on each other's hands in the game as they tried to get the riders to drop the goat carcass they were carrying towards the goal. Later, if a boy showed promise, he was given a horse and then two more.

Each trip around the country of Afghanistan was fraught with peril of some sort. On our way back from Kundus, for example, we were trapped in a late May blizzard after crossing the Salang Pass tunnel. The Salang Pass tunnel was the world's longest and highest tunnel built for the Afghans by the Soviet Union in the 1950s. The blizzard blew up so quickly that the taxi in which we were being transported became totally covered with snow. When Rebecca got out of the car, she was immediately blown about 30 feet, perilously close to the edge of a cliff. The only way we survived this ordeal was by alternately taking turns walking in front of the cab, tethered by a rope so we wouldn't fall off the cliff. We endured this walk for about four hours until we were safely down to an altitude that allowed us enough visibility to drive.

I rented a house in Paghman, 2700 feet higher than Kabul's 6000 ft. altitude. The first summer it was used for just that, a summer home to get out of the heat of the valley. I moved the horses up there and we began a pattern of going up in the late afternoon, enjoying a horseback ride and having dinner in Paghman. The next morning, another horseback ride and afterward we'd return to the Kabul house. We always kept a couple of very gentle horses for guests to ride at Paghman. One of the horseback rides in Paghman led us once again into a life and death situation.

Rebecca had made the acquaintance of a woman who was attached to the United Nations delegation in Afghanistan and claimed to be a good horseback rider. She was invited to join us on one of our rides. Unfortunately, due to her lack of skill, she had to walk the horse for about 45 minutes on the way back to the Paghman house. This got us back very late in the evening and we wanted to stay another night in Paghman before returning to Kabul. But, the U.N. lady insisted she must get back for an event that was "pressing beyond compare." I went to the tiny town square and, going outside my usual channels, found a car and driver to take us down the hill.

When the U.N. lady, Rebecca, Kachook, and I began to get into his vehicle, the driver insisted that I put Kachook into the trunk. I absolutely refused, of course. He acted concerned and looked over his shoulder most of the way down the mountain as I kept reassuring him that Kachook was just a puppy.

At the bottom of the hill on the road from Paghman to Kabul, there is a no-man's land for about 5 miles before you hit the outskirts of town. Suddenly there was some talk of gas or some car problem. The driver made a sharp right and bumped off the highway for a hundred yards or so, winding up in an encampment populated by what I can only describe as a band of nomads and desperadoes. I immediately heard him start to say, "They are rich and no one knows they are here," which he repeated in a demonic voice and then said, "We can kill them and rob them." We were forced to get out of the car and I was tackled by one of the group. We were fighting for our lives when Kachook came flying through the open backseat window and I heard the most fearsome snarl that I have ever heard coming from any animal. It got everyone's attention when he latched on to the arm of the man nearest to where he landed, nearly tearing it off. They backed off for a second. The driver screamed, "He's just a puppy" and they began to make their move again, when Kachook nailed another of the thieves by the leg, nearly breaking his ankle. This diversion allowed me to get my bowie knife from its

sheath and I grabbed Kachook by the collar while backing down toward the main highway with the women behind me. The murderers moved and started arguing with our driver – "You said he was just a puppy," "He's got a big knife," "Nobody knows they're here," "Let's circle around him," "I don't want that dog to bite me again, I'm bleeding." It was a chaos of attempts to figure out a way to encircle us as we backed and backed and backed away some more with my big knife and snarling, foaming, big, bad puppy!

God sent us a blessing in the form of a big truck that had pulled off the road and onto the little path that the taxicab had taken when we exited the highway. The truck driver had the interior light on and appeared to be looking at a map. The next thing he knew he had two women, a guy with a big knife and a huge dog clamoring into his cab, all yelling "Drive, drive!!" while the puppy, Kachook, was snarling back at the would-be murderers.

The thieves pounded on the doors of the truck and, knowing that his life might be in danger as well, the truck driver floored the thing and we drove off to the relative safety of Kabul and our house. The U.N. lady, pale and trembling, left us for her appointment. Rebecca and I swore to Kachook that we would love and protect him for the rest of his life for saving ours.

Chapter Fourteen

"I can mend the break of day
Cure a broken heart and
Provide temporary relief to nymphomaniacs."
LARRY LEE

I received a telegram at Kabul Post Restante that buckled my knees. My gentle, kind Uncle Kenny had come down with some sort of silent killer disease that couldn't be explained. A half-dozen of my relatives signed the telegram urging me, for my own personal health, to return to America as fast as I could to be tested for whatever it was that had afflicted my uncle. Rebecca and I made plans to leave. Montreal Michael took over the house and we embarked on a trip back to a place that had become virtually unknown.

It was strictly a matter of speculation, accompanied with much apprehension, as to what deadly virus, or hereditary element or genetic time bomb I might have going off. Telephones were a luxury. Calls placed to the U.S. from Nepal, Afghanistan, India, or anywhere in central Asia, required a twenty-four hour advance booking. Calls were "routed up" one day and then you returned the next day hoping that the call could be completed and that the person you were calling would not be tying up the phone line! If you got a busy signal it was another twenty-four hour wait.

We had to get off the plane in Hawaii. Rebecca became very sick on the flight and needed a break. I was anxious and eager to take advantage of the reliable U.S. phone system to find out what was up with my Uncle Kenny.

What I found out was that my uncle had Huntington's chorea, or Woody Guthrie's disease as it is commonly known. I learned I had no chance of contracting the disease. My father had already received the results of a spinal tap and the disease was not in his line of the family. Our mild panic passed.

We abandoned our hurried trip to the mainland and decided to stay in Maui to relax and decompress. Thus began our love affair with the Hawaiian Islands. We met a gentleman of Hawaiian/Chinese ancestry whose family owned a ranch that surrounded the Seven Sacred Pools out near Hana. This chance meeting, which led to a conversation about horses, accompanied by a couple of pictures of me and mine in Afghanistan, eventually earned us an invitation to stay at their place, ride their horses and visit the Seven Sacred Pools. Naturally, we accepted their hospitality and had one great experience.

The morning that we arrived at the ranch to ride, we noticed a guy painting a sign at the entrance to the adjacent ranch. Tall and handsome and smiling at us through periwinkle blue eyes, Andrew Annenberg was beginning his work. He was the recipient of the Lindbergh Scholarship and he was living in a cottage that had once been owned by the famed aviator, Charles Lindbergh and his wife, Ann. After the sensational kidnapping and trial of the 1930s, the Lindberghs retired to the Hana corner of Maui and built, in the New England tradition, an artist's cottage on the property. Through the foundation established by Lindbergh, each year an artist was awarded a scholarship that included living in the cottage and receiving a stipend. Andrew Annenberg held that award the year we met him.

When we returned from our ride to the Seven Sacred Pools, we saw the completed sign that he had created for the ranch. It was an astounding, incredible work of art. Andrew shared the story of his artistic blessings and the gift he had been given.

Andrew invited us to a party in Hana that night at the home

of a local farrier, Cowboy Rick, and his wife, Pamela Jean. The gathering attracted a nice mix of folks who had grown up in the rainforest-like eco-system as well as several new-age émigrés. As the evening spun on Rebecca remarked to me, in private, that her intuition told her that Andrew, as he went along in life, "would be spoiled by women like Picasso was." Andrew did seem to be deep in "conversation" with Ginger, then Rainbow and Summer, Leilani . . . et al.

At the next night's party, "Maui Wowie" showed up as did "Poona Butter." As we were leaving the festivities, two generous upland farmers gave me gifts of seeds from those two strains.

Like many before us, we started talking about moving to the Islands some day soon.

When we arrived in San Francisco, Rebecca suddenly wanted to go to her mother's home for some R&R. Her younger brother arrived to escort her there. I invited him to visit us in Asia when we eventually returned and I remained in San Francisco, enjoying my time with many of my old friends around the Bay Area doing what the credo must be of anyone self employed: every night was Friday night . . . but every day was Monday morning.

Big Red Ted was back in the States from Nepal. He and Cathy had returned to the University of Wisconsin because Ted had a bout of hepatitis. As he recovered, he got a Masters degree in Tibetan studies and honed his Tibetan language skills. Cathy was creating a nice niche for her imaginative work in the U.S. Ted convinced me that we had to do something for the Tibetans in the Kathmandu Valley. Exiles were arriving daily from Tibet and living in abject poverty. Tens of thousands before them, now into a second generation, were living in mud flat, tent city, unsanitary squalor.

They had built a *gompa* and a few other dwellings, but not much had really happened to help their plight and it was largely unknown to the rest of the world. Ted told me that Tashi Dorge, fueled with the few thousand dollars that I had brokered for him as payment for his family's antique rugs, had started building apartments in Bodha, Kathmandu. About 20 Tibetan families were now housed in these dwellings. Skilled *thanka* painters and carpet weavers were attempting to recreate their artistry in Bodha. They brought with them whatever they could carry, along with stories of the horrible destruction of their monasteries and the murder of innocents.

I mused that Tibetan carpets could bring in capital which would create wealth through the increasing need for goods and services. I had a minor in business.

Ted had been involved with bringing half a dozen lamas out of Tibet, saving them from the cruel occupation. He raised money through charitable organizations, a few thousand dollars at a time, to rescue these lamas because they possessed such great historical and medical knowledge.

Ted and Cathy departed for the international flight to Kathmandu full of fervor and their spirit now occupied a part of my soul as well.

I was stunned, and my world rocked, when I discovered that Rebecca was not hale and hearty and ready to come back to the party. Instead, she informed me, she was leaving me and not returning to Asia. She'd had enough of "our" whole deal. Unexpectedly hit with that kind of news, I took it as a challenge to my very manhood and dealt with it in a silent, angry and non-communicative manner. Even so, I loved her and wanted her back. I ended the conversation by saying "at least take a couple of days and think it over." But, a couple of days passed and then a couple of more, and I didn't hear from her. I felt sad and lonely. I called her with a demanding, 24-hour ultimatum. It came and went twice.

I spent another restless night. So much invested emotionally and so much invested thousands of miles away in Asia. I gave up.

"Back on the shelf" was current vernacular for being available for dating after the end of a relationship. A girl I knew from a couple of different times and a couple of different places had mi-

Snap: Bill Wassman

grated to San Francisco with the second wave of the flower children. Bill Wassman, who had just completed a year doing lighting for one of New York City's most famous fashion photographers, took a black and white snapshot of her and me. "She's more beautiful than any of those New York City models" Bill said.

This lovely, lithe garden of fantastic-looking flora had been fertilized with women's liberation. In the past, we had met up here and there around the Bay Area. She invited me to her apartment and on the way I entertained her with a few tales about my life in Kathmandu, Amsterdam and Afghanistan. She listened while lighting up the first of many cigarettes and we started peeling the intellectual onion on a path toward the mother of pearl.

One of my favorite music albums was "The Doors" live album. My "sexual beast" dealt with the women's lib part of the evening like Jim Morrison's performance of seduction in the Doors' live rendition of "Gloria."

After walkin' down the street, up her apartment stairs and knockin' at her door, Morrison's sweet nothings consist of: "Uh huh . . . uh huh . . .uh huh . . .well, could I get to know you a little better?"

Hot House Flower: "Women should be able to . . . "

Me: "Un huh, yes."

Hot House Flower Ardent Feminist: "Women have the right to . . . "

Me: "Uh huh, my, yes! I agree with that too!"

Hot House Flower Feminist Sisterhood is Powerful: "Women demand that . . . !"

Me: "Yes, yes, yes . . . well, could I get to know you a little better?"

I don't know where G – L – O – R – I – A ' s apartment was; the Doors' song is not specific, but mademoiselle had a lovely flat in the Noe Valley section of the City. It was replete with hot tub. These tubs were wedged into apartment decks and were advertised as "cuddle tubs." It lived up to its name.

This romantic evening was followed by a second date. I discovered that she was a social worker and an educated woman. Once again I agreed to everything *au courant* in the woman's liberation movement: Pregnancy leave? Good! . . . Stay at home mothers? Bad! . . . Glass ceiling? Bad! . . . Blanket political asylum for any woman who asks? Good!

"What does the Cro Magnon think of woman firefighters?" she escalated.

"Let them pull all the hoses they want!" I enthused.

Finally she raised the bar: "What about women in combat?"

"'A bazooka in every purse' would be my campaign slogan in a run for high office!" said I, earnest and without hesitation.

I again agreed to women firefighters, pregnancy leave, asylum and women in combat.

All that being said, we were again leading to where all knuckle draggers want to go when I mumbled something about how she smoked too many cigarettes, "just an observation."

She snapped back that I had challenged her "right" to smoke and stated that it was not a privilege granted by men, it was a "right" denied women until the 1920s by controlling monsters. The discussion became more heated and worse, it escalated until I was banished into the night.

I had been on my own exactly sixteen days when Rebecca called me and wanted to get back together – the total package of back together "as if we were never, ever, actually apart." We agreed to return to Afghanistan. We were going back to our life of rugged adventure, horses and Kachook.

Malaysian Airlines was offering a deal on airline tickets via Kuala Lumpur. We decided a few days on a Malay beach would be perfect before resuming our high-desert life again.

Chapter Fifteen

"And now the tale is done
And home we steer, a merry crew
Beneath the setting sun."
LEWIS CARROLL

In the Tiamon Islands off the east coast of Malaysia, there is a small private island known as Hujong-Folong (which translates from Malay as "the rainbow's end"). The island's owner was a shipping executive stationed in Singapore. He developed the small island, 90 miles north of Singapore, as a weekend retreat for his wife and children. While we were attempting to secure passage out to the Tiamons we chanced to meet them on the pier in the cross-channel harbor town of Mersing.

The family was leaving Malaysia for the season and offered us the sole use of the island. Graciously, they took us out to Hujong-Folong and re-opened the whole Swiss Family Robinson type place. The island had been developed to the point of comfort. A bamboo plumbing system delivered fresh water right to the house. There was even a generator for refrigeration.

We were in a most delightful little paradise. There was only one caveat; two good-sized monitor lizards had the run of the beach at sunset. The creatures moved from the dry side of the island (where the house was) to the wet side for their nightly hunting. They had never been a problem, we were assured, in the 23 years the family had vacationed on the island. Each night at sunset, right on schedule, the huge lizards strolled down the beach.

We were cautioned to get off the island in a week because the monsoon season was due in two weeks. "Do not be anywhere near the East side of Malaysia during the three-month monsoon season," they warned us.

We had been instructed that when we wished to leave, we should run a blue flag up a flagpole as a signal. The native fishermen would alert the captain who had brought us out and he would set across the channel to pick us up.

We didn't have a chance to put the flag up. The monsoons came early and it started raining hard and continued. The boat showed up and the captain gave us five minutes to get on board.

Chug, chug, chug up fifteen foot waves and down – over and over again. The captain's fifteen-year-old son bailed steadily. He had a soup can. He handed one to me. Chug, chug, chug up the wave, chug, chug, chug up the next wave. Rebecca was lime green. I was bailing.

Chug, chug, chug – I'm soaking wet and bailing. Rebecca's moaning. We spot a Chinese fish trap built into the middle of the sea. The Chinese leave people out there with only basic food just to tend the trap. A boat returns every three to four months. It could be one of the loneliest and most simplistic vocations on earth. Besides drowning, ending up clinging to one of those fish traps was my greatest fear. After four hours, we hit the harbor. "Good, good, you're safe," the harbor master said to us. Rebecca and I kissed the earth.

We checked into the best hotel. We found out it might be as long as two weeks until a low tide and a lunar cycle coincided, making it possible for a dash between certain levees and roads.

Monsoons in southeast Asia mean rain, night and day, for about three months. Monsoons were as big a morale-destroying factor for the American armies in Vietnam as anything else. It is an oppressive feeling, the thought of being trapped in constant rain. But we caught a break. A cabinet minister from Kuala Lumpur had been having a tête-à-tête with his mistress at our hotel.

With nothing else to do and a command of English, he welcomed our company. The Minister made a phone call every hour on the hour. He barked in Malay and I couldn't understand anything except one word and that one word was "helicopter!" His demands for a helicopter became more strident with every phone call while my murmured encouragement become more emphatic. "Helicopter!" When one finally arrived, we were graciously offered a ride and unceremoniously deposited in the Maylasian Cameroon Highlands.

Chapter Sixteen

Rogue\\'rog\\ n (origin unknown)
1 : vagrant, tramp
2 : a dishonest or worthless person : scoundrel
3 : a mischievous person : scamp
4 : a horse inclined to shirk or misbehave
5 : an individual exhibiting a chance and unusual
inferior biological variation
WEBSTER'S NEW COLLEGIATE DICTIONARY

Back in Afghanistan, the "U.S. Steel of hash oil factories" was taking shape. Supplies from Islamabad had arrived. Slowly but surely, Michael was linking up the distilling elements, pipes and valves with the various tubes and turns. Pieces of the contraption were scattered about in three rooms of the Paghman house. In one end went the hashish pollen, out the other end – golden, honey-colored oil. Cadillac and his mad professor were allowed to witness that maiden voyage. Michael hit the switch and there it went – drip, drip, drip – golden-honey hash oil. There was probably five inches of the stuff in the first of the output containers we took outside to the front yard of the house. We smeared it on doobies and tried it in pipes. We celebrated.

Then, KABOOM!!

As it turned out, the seals just weren't tight enough. The great U.S. Steel of a hash oil distillation plant blew sky high. It gutted the interior of the home. It was frightening and we were lucky we didn't blow ourselves up to that happy hash oil island in the sky.

The police chief came over to investigate the explosion, Afghan style, two days later and with his hand out, thus allowing us time to clean up the place. The chief demanded an explanation for the obviously charred remains of the interior.

The landlord of the house accompanied the chief of police. He was a wealthy man from Kabul whose grandfather had built the home in the tradition of the British Hill Station summer retreat.

"Scoundrels and *cooz, cooz*," the police chief kept repeating – *"Gonikar nafar, horab nafar"*, Farsi for "no good, bad men and a bunch of whores." *"Buru-bahii"* he added, which means "Go quickly." In this instance, it translated more like "Get outta my face."

The landlord informed me my debt to him would begin "now!" as he reached in his pocket, and with great flourish and a slow count so that I could see the bills, handed money to the police chief.

I explained that we had no idea what happened. I suggested a lightning strike.

Chapter Seventeen

ˈA verbal contract ain't worth the paper it's written on."
SAMUEL GOLDEN, MOVIE STUDIO MOGUL

Eviction, the money required to repay the landlord and a "just to see if I could do it" attitude, along with the loss of the factory resulted in needing to return to "some sort of invisible linehopping and legal loopholing." The route went from Balkh to Kabul, to the Pakistani border and on to Karachi.

Due to my financial crunch, I personally accompanied the load, paying the baksheesh to the tribal chiefs at check points in the Khyber Pass, to customs agents at the border, and to the Afghani and Pakistani truck drivers; and then, finally, to Dutch Bob's Karachi broker.

A late-night flight, on an unpronounceable airline, got me to the land of the wooden shoes and the coffee/smoke shops. This time, Bob and I were going to do the big one. Trunks full of hash. Dutch Bob's telegram said: "500 when you are ready to do it." It was during this load that I learned the why and how of the Hollanders knack of trading in spices for centuries.

I arrived in Amsterdam airport to pick up the merchandise and was immediately escorted from the cargo area and down into the bowels of the Amsterdam airport by Dutch customs officials. After a short time, they explained to me how it was going to work. They gave me two Polaroid photos of the opened trunks in front of a sign that read "Dutch Customs Narcotics Enforcement." Then they showed me a photo of a girl who had been on board a plane coming out of Asia with a small ball of hash in her boot.

"She'll be charged with your stuff, too. Do not feel too bad for her, because she was going to get three days detention for the contraband, anyway, and now she will get the same three days for the two trunks. The paperwork will say that when our diligent customs found the small ball, they then looked through her trunks. It's just a matter of paperwork."

"As for you? You will be given some vouchers. They will entitle you to some fine dining at our best restaurants as well as a small suite overlooking the Signal Canal, both courtesy of the Royal Dutch Department of Tourism for this unfortunate mistake and delay when you entered the Netherlands. So, enjoy a few days vacation." I was never sure exactly what happened.

Dutch Bob eventually showed up and slid me a sack of guilders, and said, by way of explanation, that "a young, rookie customs agent had spoiled things, a big mistake!"

My quick, rough estimate of the international currency rate indicated that I was getting about 40% of what had been agreed upon and promised.

Bob's reason for the financial discrepancy was that there were now about 30 legal hashish-selling shops in Amsterdam. Business was expanding too rapidly for there not to be a mishap.

"They're selling T-shirts and calendars with pictures of blonde Lebanese and Thai sticks plus selling every kind of pipe and paper!" complained Bob.

"With herb, when it's burned, it's gone," he continued.

"All these years, all that ganja and hashish, gone up in smoke is having to be replaced by someone, someway and somehow" said Bob, ". . . you're lucky . . . we'll be able to do twice as much next time!"

Chapter Eighteen

You can get more with a kind word and a gun
than you can with a kind word alone."

JOHNNY CARSON

After paying off everyone who had anything coming, all my profits were going to be invested in Afghan carpets. My groundwork and previous efforts had paid off with a surge in market demand. No more sophisticated bait and switch in Amsterdam for me, but there were many who were ready to join the false-bottom suitcase parade. The contraband trade was spawning legal-loopholers galore who were more than willing to try the Amsterdam run. Word had it that the Ambassador Hotel in Bombay had false-bottom suitcase makers in all sixty rooms.

German Ted and Tory showed up at the Jangalak gate with Tory's beautiful red horse with four white socks before my return from Amsterdam. Ted had recently bought it from a soon-to-be transferred American diplomat. Tory said the diplomat claimed that the American television cowboy, Roy Rogers, had been in Afghanistan to shoot a Pamir sheep and tried to buy the horse from him. Rebecca told them I would be returning that day and she arranged for us to go horseback riding together, post-jet lag.

From Jangalak to the mountains and across the Kabul River was the National Museum of Afghanistan. Coming back next to the river, the trail led to the National University of Afghanistan. The success of the carpet business and the employment of tailors

Shopping in Jangalak Village

Artie Golub

Felicia

and the fee and care required of four horses was a local industry unto itself. Even the goat brains and the entrails I boiled up daily to supplement Kachook's diet came to be a relied upon as a source of income for the local village compound. It was, as a result, safe for our women to make this ten mile round-trip horseback ride.

Just before my taxi arrived in Jangalak, Rebecca decided to ride my big stallion, Sazz. I guess she took it as a challenge. Rebecca was able to chance an occasional horseback ride by herself because of the broad belief in the nearby villages that she was a medical doctor. Our cook, Abdul, spread this bit of dis-information.

Horse Tack Repairman

Abdul, in a sense, believed she was a doctor because she explained his wife's menstrual cycle to him. Like the majority of Afghan men who paid a dowry to wed, Abdul was forced by custom to save his money until he was about forty years of age in order to be able to buy a wife. This custom also meant that in general, the wives receiving the dowry were about twenty years of age, or younger. Abdul kept a photo of his wife in the kitchen and one day I asked how she was. This benign question lead to an emotionally sad story that she was "broken." In his language, Farsi, I asked "what's wrong?" Abdul burst into tears and said, "Every month she bleeds," and pointed. After a basic explanation to Abdul I indicated that I needed assistance and I called in my wife. I translated, Rebecca used a hand-made chart and explained "Basic Woman 101" to Abdul as well as our horseman and the old gateman's married son. The commonality of this experience created the impression that Rebecca was "doctor" in their eyes. Riding in safety through their villages was our reward.

Unfortunately, the day she decided to ride Sazz, Rebecca lost control of the horse. Fortunately, the desert trail that was accessible from our house was fairly restricted by the mountain base. Sazz galloped out of control into a nomad encampment. The horse tripped on a tent stake and Rebecca went flying, head over heels. She knocked herself out. The nomads and their women kindly helped her and calmed the skittish stallion. These compassionate people managed to get her and the horse back to our house.

I had not yet put my luggage away when I saw them and frantically questioned what had happened. I sent our eunuch off to get the only American doctor in Kabul. His diagnosis was that Rebecca had sustained a mild concussion and suggested a follow-up exam the next day. The horse suffered no injury.

There was more bad news. That same night, Billy Batman took his German Mauser pistol out of its wooden case. The case, when screwed into the handle of the pistol, converted it to a rifle-like weapon. The gun slipped out of Batman's hands, dropped to the floor, discharged and shot him in the testicles.

He chose to die. Billy's wife said it was a conscious decision.

Billy's friend, an American named Archie, who tried to help him that night, was given the lethal gun by Billy's wife asking him to get rid of it so that there would be no further complications from the American Embassy or the Afghan government. She wanted to say Billy came home wounded and disavow any knowledge of what actually happened for her own self protection.

The following day, the nomads who helped Rebecca came back to our house. We treated them as our honored guests, indebted as we were for their kindness towards Rebecca and their respect for my horse. We staged an elaborate luncheon for them in the garden. The patriarch asked for a favor. They needed a gun. I spoke the Dari type of Farsi. The patriarch spoke the Ud dialect. The difference is like that of Elizabethan English and crude American slang. Eventually, it became clear they needed a weapon for protection in a blood feud that went back many generations with another band of nomads.

During our luncheon, Archie was announced at the front gate. He informed us there would be a memorial for Billy Batman and that a gravestone had been ordered with a bat carved on it. Archie also said that he wanted to get rid of Billy's gun as a favor to the widow. And get rid of it we did.

I presented it to the head man of the tribe with very little fanfare. They, in turn, professed their indebtedness to me. My gift of a gun was worth more than my wife's life and my horse's well-being.

The Patriarch

Tashi, his wife and infant arrive

In the garden

Kelli

The Patriarch

Our Gateman

Kelli's Son

His family now owed me big time. The two oldest sons of the nomad family were named Tasi and Kelli – this spelling is as close to phonetically correct as I can get. They seconded the deepest sense of gratitude that a simple, ancient culture could hold.

Ted and Tory came the next afternoon for the previously planned horseback ride. They had accompanied Rebecca and me on many horseback rides up in Paghman village. The couple was respected by the local populace for being parents of a cute toddler and for being an economic asset in that remote mountain town. Plus, Ted and Tory's home was on the fringe of the village so that we never had to ride through the com-

The Patriarch's wife and children, and Hawaiian Corriene who was visiting that day

mercial center or near the mosque.

Now, two days after the great gun presentation to the nomads, Rebecca wanted to "get back on the horse." Ted and Tory suggested we try a new route up to the ruins of Barbar's garden. None of us had ever ventured on this trail to the ancient, decayed baths and garden terraces built by Afghanistan's famous king of yore. The gardens were located at the highest point of the Kabul Valley and, Tory said, "promised a spectacular, 360 degree view."

We passed through a crumbling arch and into a small village before winding our way up to what was indeed a spectacular setting. King Barbar may have had his wives or daughters carried in sedan chairs to his opulent gardens but the two women riding their own horses were probably a first. These two western women were cantering into a headwind blowing down from the Hindu Kush Mountains, in control of their own lives.

On our return, we had no idea that a local imam had become outraged by reports of two women on horseback. As we passed his village, we were greeted by a gang of young toughs yelling "sacrilege" and charging after us with a hail of stones. No joyful shouts from youngsters of "doctor, doctor," only "sacrilege!" and "prostitutes!" screamed at us in a killing frenzy. They tried to pull us off our horses and undoubtedly would have beaten us to death. Ted and I urged the women to flee and took on the men who ranged in age from late teens to early thirties. They attacked with sticks, bottles, and another barrage of stones. Initially, Ted and I were spared from harm because we were riding perfectly trained Buzkashi stallions. These great war horses of Genghis Khan short-charged and kicked on command. Bodies were flying. Ted and I reared our horses and went for our knives until we were sure our wives were safely out of there. Eventually, one man got hold of my leg and I was being pulled off my horse. Suddenly, my stallion reared at the sound of thunderous, echoing gun shots. The man let go of my leg and the mob froze as German Ted and I spurred toward safety, positive that the bullets were directed at us. As we turned for

home, I caught sight of Kelli, the nomad, trotting towards the hill ridge. He had Billy Batman's smoking Mauser in his hand. At full gallop, Ted and I caught up with our wives and high-stepped it home.

Early the next morning, nomad Kelli pounded on the gate. It was now very dangerous for their family. His family's caravan had already departed. We bestowed a fisful of money and every provision Abdul could pack. I gave Kelli a pair of sunglasses and an Uzbeki businessman's hat for a disguise, then gave him one of our guest horses as not only a practical gift but to conform with local custom. I took a quick photo of him on his new horse to always remember his kindness. He pointed to the pistol in his boot, shouted a blessing and cantered off.

Chapter Nineteen

"If you are a bully
treat me good
If you are a bully, a bully
treat me good
I'm like a steppin Razor
Don't cha' watch my size
I'm dangerous, so dangerous
If you wanna live
treat me good
Warning
If you wanna live, I BEG YOU, you better treat me good
I'm like a steppin, jumpin' cussin' fightin' razor
I'm dangerous!"
"STEPPIN' RAZOR," PETER TOSH

News of a French man and German woman whose rotting corpses were found on the edge of Kabul swept across the ex-pat community. Jittendra and Beth had been forced to carry hundreds of stones to the roof of their Paghman home for protection after a loyal, local teenager, had warned them that a forced eviction was coming. After they spent twenty-four hours on their roof lobbing and ducking stones, the police chief himself showed up to escort them out of town. He kept their two horses as fair payment for saving Beth from being gang-raped. Beth told us, somewhat sarcastically, that Jittendra had thanked the chief, in Farsi, for his kindness.

We no longer had our house in Paghman – not since the hash oil factory blew – yet I needed to slide through that danger zone as it was the delivery point for the Waziri stallion. It took some doing to rent a Land Rover and a horse trailer. Ghiaz, Montreal Michael, The Sizzler and I prepared ourselves for anything and everything. We did have the over-and-under weapon with one shotgun shell.

We agreed that Michael would drive the Land Rover and he and Ghiaz would stay with the gun and the car to protect both from theft. The Sizzler would accompany me and watch my back during what would undoubtedly be a round of additional haggling before the big money exchange.

"Yak lak," the price of the stallion, translated to "a hundred thousand Afghani" or $10,000 US dollars, a price someone would kill your whole family for. That amount was considered the top dollar for any stallion. The Waziri was the coveted horse of choice by the most successful commercial businessmen. Many such traders still used horses as their primary form of transportation. The Waziri could travel long distances at a very smooth gait and was highly valued for the comfort the breed inherently provided.

The four of us began heading towards the exchange location at dawn. Rebecca and I had been saved by Kachook on this same road. The night before we had heard the latest news that two brothers from Minnesota, walking around the world for peace, had been found murdered. "Walking the World for Peace" said the sign on their mule cart. The brothers were welcomed with great fanfare by the Minister of

Walking the World for Peace

Tourism. International newspapers posted a photo of them posed before their "Walking for Peace" sign and noted their idealism.

Their bodies were found in the Khyber Pass. It had been only two weeks since the media hoopla. Thieves took the donkey and the cart.

It wasn't that the tribesmen were evil, nor was there anything inherent in the people of that part of the world that turned them into desperate robbers and thieves. It's simply that a great percentage of the population was, at all times, near starvation. Thousands of souls were eking it out minute-to-minute. The final days of winter meant people were down to their last turnip. There is not much in between "nothing" and "scarcity." You might say it leads to a certain credo in that part of the world: "Homicide before Starvation."

It was not unusual to be met by a gaggle of teenage boys either curious or looking for a way to pick up a little money. And so, when three or four kids motioned us "this way" and offered to lead us to the storied horse, we followed. They took us to a high walled corral at the far edge of Paghman village. The rugged trail followed a rocky, nearly dry creek. Michael had a difficult time with the Land Rover and trailer. He and Ghiaz began the demanding task of turning the car and trailer around in such narrow circumstances.

"Come inside, he is ready for you," was my first greeting from one of the several men that I assumed had accompanied the horse breeder. But when The Sizzler tried to come in with me, he said, "We must meet with you and only you – alone." We took this to be part of the negotiation.

I was geared up and ready, ready to accept some twists and turns because of the bargaining psyche in Asia.

"I must see the horse," I insisted. One of the big wooden gates was opened enough so that The Sizzler and I could see the beautiful black head with white blaze and arced ears for which the breed is known.

Ghiaz and Michael managed to get the vehicles repositioned while the bargaining continued outside the enclosed corral. I agreed to go in and meet the man by myself, but I interjected one caveat – the money was going to be held by The Sizzler. I was not going in alone with all the money. The Sizzler couldn't speak any Farsi so I explained to him that I was going in alone. He would hold the money at the Land Rover with Montreal Michael and Ghiaz. I told them to give me only thirty seconds to yell "Okay!" If they did not hear that . . . come right in.

The moment I saw the horse I was so thrilled that I let myself relax a little and concentrated on feeding him a couple of the carrots I brought for him. I barely had the treat out of my pocket and into my palm when a half a dozen men with fighting sticks came out of the shadows and over the back wall. It was obviously an ambush and planned robbery.

Whack! I was hit on the back with a stick before I could yell anything. Whack! "Give us the money and live!!" Whack! I ran for it, dodging, ducking and taking blows with no time to even pull my bowie knife from its sheath. The Sizzler came bursting through the door. A young boy with a stick was crouched trying to find a way to participate in the action. Instantly, The Sizzler had the stick out of his hand and the kid would be lucky to escape with broken arms and ribs as hard as Sizz hit him. Sizzler then delivered a ferocious blow to the thief preoccupied with me. It whacked off his ear and opened his skull, covering him with his own blood.

I scrambled for position as Sizzler parried with a couple of assailants. I careened around a pillar in the corner where feed bags were piled and heard someone gurgling as loud as he could for assistance. It was the horse dealer and he was on the ground, tied up and gagged. I dodged another fierce blow as I realized that these guys were planning on murder, not just robbery.

I got my hands on the main perpetrator's stick, spun him and got it over his head. Once under his chin I snapped his neck. Now I had a stick but they still had us outnumbered. The Sizzler took one, then another blow.

It was then I heard the explosion. Ghiaz was standing in the doorway with our smoking shotgun in his hand. He had fired the only round into the air. He pretended to reload.

Everyone froze in their tracks. One of the robbers started pointing towards me and shouting to Ghiaz in Farsi, "You missed, you missed – shoot again, shoot the infidels!!" Ghiaz stared him down while holding the shotgun across his chest. He didn't move or say a word.

The scheme was broken. The scene shifted into a tableau of beaten men tending to their wounded.

The Sizzler wasted no time getting behind Ghiaz and pulling out his own knife. I managed to untether the horse and told them to get him in the trailer. I cut the horse breeder loose with my knife. He pointed at my bloody nose and then asked me to pay him. I did and he leaped on his own horse and galloped off without a word or a backwards glance.

I made my way back to the Land Rover as the thieves directed their curses and threats to Ghiaz. Michael drove slowly through the village with Sizz and Ghiaz in the car while I limped along behind the trailer for as long as I could manage. I wanted to go past as many of the villagers as could be seen. I did not want to have

a claim made against us alleging that we had stolen the horse and inflicted the mayhem. If the police chief showed up we were going to "kick his ass" and keep moving.

I spent three days in bed, my body totally black and blue from the beating I took; but I had the horse and Rebecca was a most loving and sympathetic nurse. It was a couple of weeks later that I received a letter from that "hot-house flower" back in San Francisco announcing, in a casual way, "I am going to have your baby in a few months." In essence, the letter said there was no doubt to the bloodline. Also, she added that I could check it out, in person, at any time . . . "and someday, if the child asks about the father, I'll just say he was the Bandit of Kabul."

There was a P.S. "I quit smoking since it's not good for kids."

Rebecca was very understanding and replied "looks like we're going to have a hostage to the future."

Chapter Twenty

"Behind every great woman there's an idiot."
JOHN LENNON

Rebecca always described the disintegration and what happened next as "While the Hookah Bubbled."

Buses full of travelers from Frankfurt, Amsterdam or London passed through Kabul every day or so. These vehicles could accommodate about eighteen hearty souls who were trying to make it to the increasingly popular "Nirvana of the East" on the same shoe-string-budget guide book. After going through the drug law dichotomy of Turkey, i.e. it being that hashish was readily available and used openly, but, if you were caught with some, you paid dearly in Turkey's infamous, draconian manner, there was paranoia at every border crossing, even if you didn't have any drugs.

Some of those hassled, half-starved road heroes found their way into the oasis that was the Sina Hotel outside of Kabul. A guy named Sakhi worked out of this hotel. He was very well connected and he sold bits of the wonderful Sharikh hash from Balkh to those travelers who passed through the hotel. Sakhi was from the Balkh area where the golden, hand-pressed hash originated. It was, as far as I was concerned, the finest that Afghanistan had to offer. He had married an attractive woman from Wales who never appeared in anything but the finest Turkoman-style clothes and jewelry. How and where they met was always a subject of dis-

Sakhi and his Welsh wife

cussion. Sakhi never shared a hint about that or anything, especially his sources and methods of dealing with the warlords of the North. While she didn't wear a scarf, Sakhi's wife was more than demure when she served her husband's guests tea.

German Ted and I were sitting in the garden negotiating with Sakhi to make a run up north to purchase a bit of hash for ourselves. German Ted had it going to Europe successfully as well. He created disks of the Sharikh hashish and put a light coating on them. Tory painted stunningly beautiful pictures of various Buddhist deities on the disks and they were, well . . . sailing through customs. Tory had taken refuge in Buddhism during her pregnancy.

Ted was rolling one of those three-paper European joints that included tobacco and a filter. While I was never particularly fond of mixing tobacco with hash, it always made for a more pleasant negotiation. German Ted and I needed each other on this particular deal because Sakhi wouldn't go unless there was a certain amount of money involved – a sum that neither Ted nor I had individually. As part of the deal, Sakhi was also demanding that Tory paint an image of a mullah on one of the hash disks.

The garden of the Sina Hotel had high, adobe walls and beautiful trees shading comfortable chaise lounges. Above us we could hear the ruckus of arrival coming from rooms full of the new, weary guests. Sakhi, Ted and I were enjoying strawberries and cream with wonderful tea when into the garden walked an obviously Nordic beauty. She was a statuesque blonde classic in her early twenties wearing a blue Turkish *rampa* shirt, long Moroccan fleece-lined suede coat, tight blue silk slacks tucked into Spanish boots. A gorgeous face glowed under a blue beret.

Mona

Danish Mona's arrival was not only the end of our hash negotiations with Sakhi, it was the beginning of the end of everything that German Ted had going for him, including his pretty, intelligent wife who loved him enough to help him smuggle hashish, who gave him a beautiful baby girl and who was willing to live in some of the wildest and most dangerous places on earth just to be by his side. It was all, as of this moment, *finito* – over and done. Ted rented a room at the Sina and began his non-stop pursuit of Mona. Tory eventually took baby Guava and left for Kathmandu.

Ted had already convinced an obviously pregnant Aggie to carry suitcases with concealed hash to Amsterdam. Ted's romantic pursuit prevailed and it wasn't long before Mona was included in this plan. Aggie's big stomach, and the fact that eight of them were making the trip, was the strategy the principals embraced. I didn't have much faith in these operations. The suitcases were built with false bottoms. The linings were glued back on, often in a very shoddy manner, plus customs officials in other countries caught someone once in a while, enroute.

Fortunately, Aggie and Mona were successful and returned to Kabul with Ted's share of the money. Unfortunately, for German

Ted, Mona's mother arrived with them. Momma accompanied her daughter to Kabul with one thing in mind: no German Ted was going to make money off of her daughter by having her carry suitcases filled with hashish to Europe.

Mona's mother was immediately dubbed the "happy hooker" because of her resemblance to Xavier Hollander, the original "Happy Hooker" who wrote sexual advice columns for *Playboy* magazine (Hollander's columns morphed into a Hollywood film of her life dispensing a bold, European type of sexual advice to American neophytes).

The Kabul ex-pat community thought Momma was there to rescue her daughter and at least scold German Ted. Instead, she was there to set it up so that Mona was running hashish for her.

Within a year's time, Mona and Momma accomplished quite a few successful runs back and forth to Amsterdam. We all welcomed them on their returns to Kabul and happily received their gifts of European culinary delights. I once suggested to them that Mona could end up in jail somehow, but Momma assured me that "no male Dutch customs agent on earth would want to do anything except have sex with Mona, period!" Momma added, emphatically, "I watch and they are always on their best behavior when Mona passes through."

Mona shrugged, "Momma bakes the apple pies and off we go!"

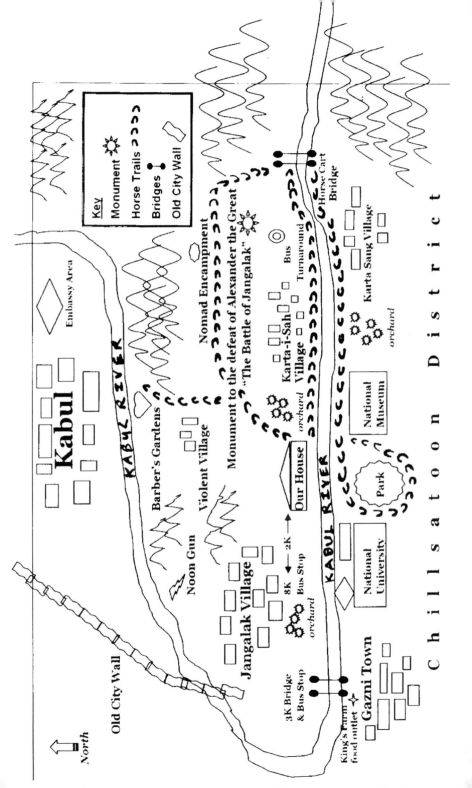

Chapter Twenty-One

"You don't have to answer
There's no need to speak
I'll be your belly dancer, prancer
And you can be my Sheik."
"MIDNIGHT AT THE OASIS," AS PERFORMED BY MARIA MULDAR

At our home in Jangalak, Abdul cooked dinner for ten every night. Guests who attended were ardent conversationalists, intellectuals and artists. The evenings were alive with entertainment and merriment. Some played local instruments, others acoustic guitars. Our home became an ever-changing showplace for the treasures we would buy and sell. Rebecca was a walking

Party attendees Susie and Arnie and Baltimore Billy

manikin, resplendent in the clothes and jewelry she found in the bazaar or had sewn by our tailors.

Alejandro was released from the Afghan prison and came over to say a fast goodbye. I owned a hookah that was six feet tall – you had to stand on a small stool to be able use it in the proper fashion. The bowl was so big that it required three ounces of hashish placed under charcoal briquettes to fire it properly. We brought it out on this occasion to celebrate Alejandro's freedom. He was "in love with the world" as Rebecca described him.

Our festive group was enjoying William VIII performing on the balalaika when suddenly there were whistles and noises and a commotion such as we had never heard before.

I ran to the second floor window and saw boys with red scarves around their necks coming over the walls of our compound. Through the twilight, I could see someone in an Afghan officer's uniform, also wearing a red scarf around his neck. He was berating the gateman. It was about 100 yards from the house to the giant castle-like gates that secured our estate. Abdul went down to the front stairs to find out what was up. The gates were thrown open and two more military uniforms and another half dozen red-scarfed youths rushed through. "Passports, passports," the officer kept shouting. In fluent Farsi, I yelled "What's the problem?" The military men explained to me that there was a new government in Kabul and a new day for Afghanistan and that he wanted our passports. Now assembled in the compound were a dozen or so young cadres, each carrying a machete or a fighting stick. The gateman was screaming and crying. Abdul charged out of the house, waving his arms and injecting obscenities into his threat that the property owner was the Deputy Prime Minister and he spat out the details of all the bad things that were going to happen to them for this disturbance. My loyal horseman, Asmir, shouted and yelled for them to go away from his quarters next to the horse barn. They started threatening back. The young officer ordered a half a dozen cadres on to Abdul. They violently dragged him down.

By then, Rebecca and the guests at the party had found their way to windows and the edge of the balcony. The thugs pulled Abdul down on the ground. One of them dove at him and slowly, right before our eyes, gnawed off his little finger and handed it to the officer. The officer held up the bloody stump, looked me in the eye and said, "I want the passports – NOW!" I, of course, told him "yes." And that was it, the rush was on. Our exodus from Afghanistan began. We were given 72 hours to get out of the country.

Once again lives were twisted with weapons, threats and violence in the name of politics. What was occurring was a coup that overthrew the King of Afghanistan. The King's cousin, Daoud, ascended to the post of prime minister and abolished the monarchy. Daoud was a long-time symbol of Afghani democracy. He had been prime minister during a period when the country had flirted with a constitutional monarchy. Daoud expressed his democratic views once too often, though, and his cousin threw him in jail. He continued to be popular with students; the guys in the red bandannas were young, political democrats. Obviously, Daoud was the choice of some factions in the Afghan military. The military officer holding Abdul's bloody finger above his head, barking orders, was the most recent symbol of the ever-changing quicksand of Asian politics.

After the melee, Rebecca tended to the wounded Abdul and the first thing I had to do was to find the right homes for our horses. Ghiaz, who had been the deciding factor during the attempted horse robbery was, like all Afghans, an expert horsemen and kindly helped me place my horses into the best existing herds. I had to get an airplane-worthy crate built to ship Kachook back with us. Sakhi and his wife took our beloved cat, Sammy.

Great sadness prevailed during those final hours with the staff. They faced an uncertain future after finding, with us, a modicum of stability in their lives. We packed the Afghan carpets, tapestries and one-of-a-kind treasures and got everything shipped to the States; what we didn't ship, we carried with us.

It was pandemonium at the Kabul airport. Customs was nonexistent and everything was shipped or loaded without much concern for what was going out. The old system of baksheesh still worked wonders with the new regime.

Kachook left Afghanistan with Rebecca's brother, Evan, who happened to be visiting us at the time of the coup. Our dog had no papers other than a certificate for his rabies shot from The Royal Afghan Veterinary clinic. Both dog and brother managed to make the journey to the U.S.A. intact, although Kachook and Evan spent two nights in the London airport, quarantined, until someone got tired of it all. Kachook was a big dog, loved his food and the airport offered many inspired places to relieve himself. Evan was allowed to take Kachook out for walks but he was not allowed to leave the grounds, so what's a dog to do? Eventually the customs officials declared that they were America's problem and sent them on to New York. When Evan and Kachook got to New York City, word of the coup in Afghanistan had reached customs. The customs agent, amazingly, just let Evan and the dog go through.

I made a last pass at Post Restante and without looking through all the mail, stuffed it in my bag.

Eventually there weren't enough planes. The foreigners were in mass flight, via Herat into unpleasant Iran or chancing the Khyber Pass. Rebecca and I, like Alexander the Great before us, were officially and unceremoniously kicked out of Jangalak and joined the exodus. William VIII and Aggie were the only exceptions because Aggie was ready to deliver their son. He was the first foreigner born in a monarch-less Afghanistan.

Rebecca and I planned to return to the States in the opposite direction as her brother and Kachook, after we made a business stop in Thailand. We were heading toward California and San Francisco, starting out by going overland through the Khyber Pass and spending a night in Jalalabad, a city on the old southern crossing route. Jalalabad was edgy, noisy and sounds of scattered violence kept us awake all night long.

We managed to reach the other side of the Khyber Pass in a 1953 Chevrolet station wagon that we paid a Pakistani driver a fortune to drive for us. The car was listing hard right because the shock absorbers were nonexistent and we loaded the car with everything we could carry. A small, railroad-crossing type gate was all that marked the Pakistan/Afghanistan border. The horizon offered desert and dunes as the chugging chore for our vehicle.

We were limping through the barren flatlands towards civilization when suddenly, from out of everywhere, jeeps with machine guns mounted on the back surrounded us. Our driver seemed unconcerned and came to a stop. We had four machine guns pointing at us. Through the swirling dusk came a Pakistani officer sporting a full handlebar moustache, riding jodhpurs, pistol on his hip and his riding crop in hand. At full attention, he announced "Pakistani Mobile Anti-Smuggling Patrol" in perfect English.

"Good late afternoon to you, officer," I replied.

He leaned over and peered into the car and smiled broadly when he saw Rebecca in the back seat. He stood again at full attention and said, "And good afternoon to you, madam. I am sorry to trouble you, but I must ask you – do you have any hashish?"

"Of course not," chimed Rebecca, sitting in the midst of boxes and suitcases in the back seat of the Chevy.

"Carry on, then," he answered with a soft salute. It's a nice feeling when machine guns leave. Only the lurch forward of the beat-up Chevy could disturb our life-affirming kiss.

Our Gardener

Archie and Donna with German Ted's Puppy

Fred and Maybee

Montreal Michael and Evan

Big Anne or Big Linda

William VIII, Aggie and their son in Front of Kabul Hospital. In the final exodus Aggie and William's son was born two days after the forced deportation

Chapter Twenty-Two

"I lay traps for troubadours who get killed
before they reach Bombay."
"SYMPATHY FOR THE DEVIL," THE ROLLING STONES

When we finally arrived in San Francisco, I purchased a converted school bus known as the "Oakie Drifter." "The Drifter" had been tricked out to comfortable perfection by its previous owner and it was large enough to carry everything we managed to get out of Kabul. We located Rebecca's brother Evan and enjoyed a cheerful reunion with him and our dog, Kachook. Rebecca, Kachook and I then headed out to buy some water. Specifically, land with water on it. A small pond, a bend in a river or a swimmin' hole. We went to Oregon and Washington before finding a blessed piece of the planet in the foothills of Northern California.

William VIII and Aggie sent aerograms from Kabul to announce the birth of their son. Since most souls had been rudely scattered, we didn't get the news for a month and by then we had received less welcome news.

William VIII and Aggie took their newborn baby and headed to the Swat Valley in the tribal area of Northwestern Pakistan. Only a few hard travelin' types made it to Swat. Tribal territories were known to be even more dangerous than Afghanistan. The Wali of Swat was only slightly beholden to the political structure of Pakistan. Pakistani federal power meant paperwork, rubber stamps and fees that were necessary to stay more than three days. William VIII rented a decent house, hired a servant and went to Peshawar to get the visa for his family. He was found dead in his hotel room.

The American Embassy and Pakistani officials quickly called it a "heart attack." A distraught Aggie and the infant were hustled off to the U.S. On her return, she told us the shocking news even before their birth announcement arrived.

After a series of murders along the hashish trail were tied to Charles Gurmukh Sobhraj, we all rethought 25-year-old William VIII's much too young and healthy "heart attack." Sobhraj's *modus operandi* was to befriend fellow travelers before killing and robbing them of their passports and travelers checks. His road of death spanned France to Kathmandu. He killed three people in Swayambunath shortly after arriving in Nepal. He poisoned many of his victims after meeting them around the hotel or traveler's restaurants. William VIII's sad demise seemed similar and coincided with Sobhraj's known travel timeline. Everything William VIII owned was gone, but that was attributed to thieving, corpse-robbing hotel employees. Everything about the nature of his death was troubling and unresolved.

Chapter Twenty-Three

After thirteen years in an insane asylum in Washington, D.C. the poet Ezra Pound was asked how it went. "Rather badly. But in what other place could one live in America?"

We found refuge at a decrepit hot spring health spa that was popular in the 1930s. A horseback riding girlfriend of Rebecca's, Penny Nichols, was renting one of the last, livable, ramshackle cabins on the spa grounds while stabling her two horses in a converted garage. After driving the Oakie Drifter night and day for a couple of months, I was ready to soak.

An old, local cowboy asked me if I wished to take a ride with him up the canyon while he scouted stray cattle. He said I'd see a 200-year-old Spanish-made stacked stone corral that was still used during spring season branding. Once out of the flatland silt, the creek we were following to the foothills became crystal clear. Two hours ride past the stone corral I spotted a hand-lettered sign tacked to a fence post planted on a fire break that read "ranch for sale." I called out to the old cowboy, "What kind of ranch is it?"

"A ranch with no fences, gates, or cattle – just a creek, really, and some waterfalls," he yelled back at me with a laugh, adding, "It's more of a damn farm!"

On closer inspection the property encompassed a thirty-five foot waterfall as well as a nine-foot waterfall and three other swimmin' holes. On a true southern slope, at 2,500 feet, it had a direct view to the Yuba Buttes forty-five miles away.

I bought it.

It was known as Dirty Creek and that was a misnomer. The creek had been named by local folks down in the flatlands where it flowed after picking up a lot of the foothill silt. That was a very big break. Imagine you're driving down Interstate 5 in your huge RV with a slew of kids and you want to go camping. Would you choose Rock Creek, Deer Creek, Pine Creek, Crystal Creek or . . . Dirty Creek?

Chapter Twenty-Four

"It is not a question of how much we know, how clever we are, nor even how good; it all depends upon the heart's love. External actions are the results of love, the fruit it bears; but the source, the root, is in the deep of the heart."

"The Inner Life," Francois Fenelon 1651-1715
printed 1853 English translation

I first soloed in a Cessna 172 model airplane on January 7, 1970, and I flew every day thereafter for a week. For a season, I parlayed my limited skills into a "Johnny Potseed" pilot, flying short hops around the Emerald Triangle.

Years later, when settled on the ranch, we turned that small plane-flying skill into nice, romantic interludes. Our idea of modern romance was to fly, Alaska bush-pilot-style, to a restaurant, where after landing, they picked you up in a scale model steam train. The restaurant was named the Nut Tree and was an equal forty-five miles from Sacramento and San Francisco. It was allegedly created so that the power brokers could meet halfway between the California State Capitol and the big money in the Bay Area to arrange those "side" deals that had to be discussed mouth-to-ear only. Adding the airstrip cut the bigwigs' travel time to the restaurant's expansive grounds. The Nut Tree's airstrip was the shortest in California. I knew how to fly a small plane but did not have a license or much in the way of navigator skills. A new friend who owned the puddle jumper rented it to me under the false assumption that I actually had a pilot's license.

On one luncheon outing, it took me three passes at the small strip to get the plane down, which upset Rebecca's enjoyment of one of the Nut Tree's splendid nouvelle California culinary presentations.

Gnoss Field, the field where I originally learned to fly, is one of the most difficult small plane airstrips to land on in California. It is surrounded by swamp and wetlands on three sides and a freeway on the other. A fierce crosswind blows off the ocean with increasing strength almost every afternoon. I learned to fly at Gnoss Field, surmising that if I could learn there, most other air strips would be easy. I was planning on landing in the middle of the Mojave Desert after a little jump up from Mexico anyway. I quickly learned to fly the plane and work the radio, but my navigational skills were shaky at best.

It had been wind sailor Skipper Gary's idea to cross those invisible border lines by using a small plane and it was he who encouraged me to take those initial flying lessons. His idea developed in connection with his ownership of a recreational vehicle that he had converted to carry contraband.

I met Skipper Gary on the Sausalito waterfront when he was ferrying supplies to the Native Americans occupying Alcatraz Island. Currently, he had been hired as a master woodworker on David Crosby's sailboat, "The Maya." The pop music star, Crosby, had a home in nearby Mill Valley. I had great admiration for Crosby because of his activist efforts in the anti-Vietnam War movement. Crosby, it was known, had hidden in the trunk of a car for fifty dangerous miles through a violent, right-wing gauntlet to perform at an Austin, Texas, war protest. Now, Crosby was eschewing the Hollywood lifestyle after he'd been fired from the hit-making band, The Byrds, and had formed the super group CSN. Skipper Gary got me on board "The Maya" for a sail on San Francisco Bay with Crosby. Afterwards we moored outside the Trident Restaurant in Sausalito.

The Trident was the hotbed hangout of marijuana smugglers, dealers and rock stars. The waitresses at the Trident were allowed to wear whatever they wanted, rather than some sort of pink fluffy uniform or bunny outfit, which was in vogue at that time. Crosby, Skipper Gary and I ordered food outside on the deck of the restaurant. Seated at the table next to us were four black men. It was Miles Davis and he was with two older gentlemen, and one young man in his late teens. Crosby stood up and gushed, "You're Miles Davis, man. You're my hero and the most incredible musician going today." He was sincere and truly heartfelt. It was at that moment that I began to truly like David Crosby, for his genuineness and openness.

Miles looked over at Crosby, dropped his sunglasses down his nose, peered over them and didn't say a word. The two older men frowned and oozed distain. It was as if the three of them were directing little sparks and bad vibes at Crosby. Nonetheless, Crosby stammered on, talking about particular pieces of Davis' music and how brilliant it was, as well as throwing in the fact that they had appeared on the same stage in New York City once. Miles still didn't say a word. Suddenly, the young black teenager sitting with the three said to them, "You guys don't know who this is . . . this is David Crosby . . . he's got hits." Then to David he said, "Don't pay no attention to these guys, man. These old men, they don't know nothin' about your band." He pointed adamantly to David and said to his three companions, "These guys don't know race! They're hippies! They love everyone, man."

"And you've got hits!" the young man concluded. "Don't pay attention to these old men, they're from a different time."

I never knew if he was a relative of Miles or what, and why he was able to make comments like this to a known, cool legend, but it was an amazing moment in time.

All praise to Miles for being a decent human being and a truly great musician with a good heart. He recorded the Crosby song "Guinevere" shortly thereafter, which as much as anything else, established David Cosby as an artist and not just a pop star.

A love of flapping canvas, the whistling wind and salt spray was born in me that day. I gave up flying noisy, motorized aircraft and switched to gliders. The money-making opportunities a glider offered were practically nil, but weighed against silent soaring, eye-to-eye with red-tailed hawks, it was worth a king's ransom.

The romantic 100-mile hops down to the Nut Tree ended when a small plane crashed on the restaurant's tiny airstrip while Rebecca and I were dining. In attempting to find out what happened I asked an official on the scene, who said "Minor case of wind shear . . . happens out here on the prairie regularly" and then added succinctly: "People either know how to fly or they sorta know how to fly."

He then said, pointing toward the smoking wreckage: "That guy sorta knew how to fly."

Rebecca and I enjoyed an expensive, yet very romantic, 100-mile taxi ride home.

Chapter Twenty-Five

"I'm tired of looking at the TV news
I'm tired of driving hard and paying dues
I figure baby, I've got nothing to lose
I'm tired of being blue
That's why I'm going to Kathmandu
kkkkkkk Kathmandu"
"Kᴀᴛʜᴍᴀɴᴅᴜ," Bᴏʙ Sᴇɢᴇʀ & ᴛʜᴇ Sɪʟᴠᴇʀ Bᴜʟʟᴇᴛ Bᴀɴᴅ

"**S**potted Horse International," was the name of the business I set up to support our lifestyle. I hired an international tax advisor, accountant and customs brokers on both ends and, as if ordained, the enterprise started rolling from day one. The business revolved around three kinds of Tibetan carpets. The first type was made of yak hair, using only natural dyes. I felt consumers would eventually find the value in this carpet because it could last for about 100 years. The second type was a unique style that came from a region on the outskirts of Lhasa called "Walloon." This style evolved in the 1950s. It was sort of the "shag carpet" for middle-class Tibetans with colorful dyes and wild non-traditional designs. The Walloons are best described as a clan living in accordance with the Buddhist philosophy. They had relocated from Tibet to a remote corner of the accessible pass between Bhutan and Nepal when the Dalai Lama fled in exile. The third type of carpet I specialized in was the Tibetan Tiger design. Meditating on Tiger carpets is said to give the power of the tiger to the meditator. Over the centuries, the Tiger carpet evolved into many representations of the animal. Tibet had no tigers, thus they were depicted at various times in history as elaborate, colorful profiles, splayed pelts or even a bare bones skeleton with a head and whiskers.

Our great hope was that the money earned from these sales would help lift the Tibetan exiles and refugees in Nepal out of their mud hovels and hellholes. When the first big shipment left for the States we rewarded ourselves with a trek to the Annapurna Sanctuary.

President Richard Nixon offered the King of Nepal $200 million to build a sewer system for the capital city of Kathmandu. The string that was attached to this bribe was that the Kingdom of Nepal would then become the last country in the world to finally criminalize ganja. No less than the soon-to-be disgraced Vice President Spiro T. Agnew, while in Nepal to negotiate the deal, had actually stopped his entourage at the Inn Eden in Kathmandu. Its small sign, an open advertisement for hashish sales on the second floor, caught the vice president's attention. All this bravado, just so he could point out to his Nepalese diplomatic hosts the unacceptability of this little shop. Agnew berated his host about this and, combined with the $200 million, Nepal got on board. A country that had no heroin junkies or opium dens at the time would become overrun with them. In Nepal, hashish use was an integral part of religious ceremonies. For 1500 years it had been part of the culture and was embedded in acceptable society. Hash offered no beacon to criminals and thugs. Making it "illegal" created a new market for not only hashish but other illegal substances and the days of relaxed smoking and social highs were gone forever. The $200 million was wonderful seed money for criminal enterprises.

Within a year, in order to add credence to the necessity of making hashish illegal, a nasty rumor was spread. The rumor was that Henry Kissinger himself, using American Express traveler's checks, had bought two kilos of pure heroin in Durbar Square in downtown Kathmandu. Anyone who was there at the time knew that this was utter nonsense.

Simultaneously, the Tibetan carpet bonanza was on. As the carpets sold, the Tibetans purchased Levis, Levis jackets and cassette players. Honda 90 motorcycles zipped around everywhere. The brick factories went night and day to supply the Bohda apartments being constructed. Fifty meters from Ted and Cathy's gate, above the Bodnath stupa, a small, 500-year-old dharamsala encircled a beautiful old shade tree. It became the location of a "financial futures" market based on carpet sales. I enjoyed Ted's descriptive letters detailing how it blossomed into a full-blown mini-Wall Street exchange, based on the international money-grams that I sent periodically.

Conversely, the ex-pats were starting to eat the easily available opium. Too many were attempting to emulate the hashish smuggling past. Off-the-wall schemes and the aptly named "pipe dreams" were disastrous and usually ended with time in jail for the would-be smuggler. Rebecca accused me of making it look too easy.

One such scheme sent thirteen women, each carrying two false-bottom suitcases, simultaneously out of the same travel agency in Kathmandu, to Australia. The brilliant part of this scheme was that the runners would go via Nairobi, where they would all claim to have had their passports stolen by their "missing" tour leader. Armed with new passports issued in Kenya, they and their suitcases would be welcomed, easily, in Australia. Of course, they were all arrested as soon as they got there.

Another crazy scheme involved building hash-carrying cages for two Lesser Pandas. The rare creatures immediately attracted the attention of customs officials. Tibetan mastiff puppies were shipped in similar hash-concealing cages and eventually snatched by customs authorities in the United States. It made for colorful journalistic reporting in the *International Herald Tribune*. The tyrannical, old-line enforcement apparatus employed these bizarre tales as propaganda to bash all the countries of Asia into "quota" arrests.

Chapter Twenty-Six

"If the President does it, it's not illegal."
RICHARD M.NIXON,
THIRTY-SEVENTH PRESIDENT OF THE UNITED STATES, 1969-1974

Those of us who were old enough voted for Lyndon B. John-son. He was the "Peace Candidate." The "Peace" Candidate. If we would have known his later publicized recipe for political success: "Accuse your opponent of f***ing pigs then watch him deny it," we may have made another choice.

When Big Red Ted finished his studies at the University of Wisconsin, he and Cathy returned to Nepal and found a fantastic home in Bodha. It was an old Rana palace built high on a knoll above the Bodha Stupa. It was similar to our Jangalak place, being located on a couple of acres behind surrounding high walls. Soon a dozen full-time Nepalese and Tibetans were employed at the house and it became a force in the local economy. Ted and Cathy had two Lhasa Apso pups from a bloodline originating in Tibet. Ted had a little corner plot in the garden that he tended himself which yielded what he called "Bodha Blue." It was grown with seeds from my developing purple strain at the ranch but the high Himalayan light gave it a bluish hue.

Even the taciturn Bill Wassman was in high spirits as we all celebrated at the Chong Shop when, as the new President Gerald Ford said "the long American nightmare is over." It was during one of my frequent trips to Nepal that Bill Wassman showed up in

Kathmandu, much to the relief of his wife Patty. He was on assignment in New York City and made a brief stop in one of his old haunts in Ibiza before heading back to Asia.

The next morning we rode the horses up to Zena's monastery on Karpon Hill where we were always offered tea by Lama Yeshe and Zopa.

An easy glimpse into each of these four friends would be to

As the caricature states: Bill and Patty Wassman shared the same birthday.

describe their sense of humor. Big Red Ted could find humor in almost anything and enjoyed provoking an even funnier response and joining in the laughter. His wife, Cathy, had a hearty,

Bill
Jerry
Rebecca
Kathy
Red Ted
at Old
Rana
Palace

Photo Patty Wassman

genuinely feminine bellow. Patty Wassman always giggled into her shoulder. A funny anecdote from her was witty and well told. Bill was a compassionate ironic. He chuckled progressively louder and longer as his audience "got" the pathos and tragedy that almost always oozed from him. Rebecca was a sincere audience, who rarely spoke, but almost always with comic insight kept the dialogue going. Her eyes would sparkle.

Big Red Ted arranged a well-planned, well-thought out and well-provisioned trek up to the Annapurna Sanctuary. It is one of the most beautiful parts of Nepal; it is sacred to the ancient Bon religion of the Garung inhabitants who later adopted Tibetan Buddhism.

Big Red Ted had been organizing on-the-fly-for-friends trekking expeditions in Nepal with great success for all. He had created a team of fantastic Tibetan and Sherpa guides, cooks and porters. At Ted's suggestion, I shipped a trunk full of modern mountaineering equipment, supplies and provisions to Nepal. This time our adventure would be a lot more comfortable and much healthier, food-wise, than relying on the local harvest. We had a memorable venture to the ice caves of the Annapurna Sanctuary. Rebecca handled it like a deer caught in the headlights. But it was so exhilarating for me that I went out on the Everest trek after a week's rest. Ted understood and since he loved trekking so much, he decided to make it his living.

Humpayetti Trekking Company came to life. Bill Wassman took some enticing photos and I wrote the following for the illustrated brochure:

How about some adventure in a country with none of the tensions of western civilization? Where crossing the street in the capital may mean traveling back 200 years in time? Where cars have to slow down and edge carefully around a sacred cow lying peacefully in the middle of the road?

Lace up your hiking boots and walk up to an entirely different world populated by Tibetans and Sherpas and animals such as yaks and snow leopards. A mystic land of hidden valleys and a belief in the mysterious 'yeti' or abominable snowman. Let's go find some healthy, hearty fun in Asia.

Nepal is a small kingdom lodged between India and China that has endured most likely because geographically it consists primarily of the Himalayan mountain range, home of Mount Everest, the world's highest mountain.

Trekking is not mountain climbing. Trekkers stay below the snow and ice level and equipment such as high survival gear, foot crampons and ice picks are not necessary.

Besides Everest, another popular choice with many spectacular and exhilarating views as well as culturally interesting village life and monasteries on the way up and down is the Annapurna Sanctuary. Three peaks named Annapurna I, II and III as well as a mountain known as Machapuchare form this part of the range, and many experienced mountaineers call these peaks the most beautiful in the world.

Kathmandu, a charming, sprawling city of low roofs, brick buildings and narrow streets filled with water buffalo carts, rickshaws and colorful bazaars is the capital of Nepal. Everything begins here including the necessity of obtaining a trekking permit from the proper government office.

As you walk your body gets stronger and acclimated. The mind has time to dwell on the beauty of nature and you meet wonderful local people (often the legendary high altitude dwellers, the Sherpas.) You will admire their toughness, strength and cheerful friendliness. Ancient monasteries clinging to rock buttresses appear. The monks are smiling, spiritual and happy to offer a blessing or provide a bit of shelter or tea.

The adventurer often happens on village festivals for everything from harvest, holidays, weddings or fertility. These are colorful costumed affairs and always quite joyous and interesting observations of ancient forms of dance or gay, noisy celebration.

Above the villages, the streams run clear and sparkling. The summits thrust toward the sky with their knife-sharp saw-tooth ridges and whipping plumes of snow. Sunsets are bigger, closer . . . crimson and gold.

People the world over have looked to the mountains for inspiration and spiritual refreshment. Each time I have trekked has been just as exciting and stimulating as the first.

Chapter Twenty-Seven

"When I get lonely and I'm sure I've had enough
She sends her comfort coming in from above
We don't need a letter at all
We got a thing that's called radar love."
"RADAR LOVE," GOLDEN EARRING

Patty left Bill Wassman. It was a minor miracle of the ages that she hadn't left him sooner. One of the reasons that Bill had become one of the world's greatest travel photographers is that he was willing to take a treacherous bus ride up any mountain in Asia, or live in the backwater of an unheard of island in the Philippines, or risk a voyage in a narrow, canoe-like river craft up the Irrawaddy, in Burma. "Anytime, anyplace, anywhere" said Bill. He was willing to eat lizards, roots, snakes or whatever was eaten whereever in the world he went. Bill never cared much about food. He cared about the photo. He was true to Socrates in the short form: "Eat to Live!" For Patty, those water-logged, rusting hulks that served as inter-island ferries, or chugging diesel buses that broke down in the middle of nowhere, were no longer exotic, interesting or romantic.

I would remind everyone that when we were roommates postcollege, Bill would cook up a mess of tripe, potatoes, carrots and cabbage in a big pot, simmer the concoction for about twelve hours, and eat it for three meals a day for five days in a row. It was as if he was preparing himself, then, for the life he would lead in Asia, a life that that brought us the beautiful photographs of those remote realms. He captured time and place, mood and space. Bill's work in photography was similar in feeling to the paintings of Andrew Annenberg on Maui (we cherished the photos

Andrew sent us after an arduous year painting single-hair-brush style).

By the next year, Nepal was rapidly becoming a different place from the Nepal we had experienced earlier in the decade. Hippies had originally come to Nepal hitchhiking overland and by train and bus out of Europe on journeys that were not unlike pilgrimages. Traveling slowly out of the modern life of Western civilization and into the ancient world of Asia somehow acclimated the traveler. Western focus turned to Eastern philosophy and our understanding of local customs and traditions dawned, for most of us, by simply taking our time and "going with the flow." This acclimation included a trade-off of modern life's stresses and values. It took all our energy to handle the stress of everyday life traveling in Asia. Experiences that would crumble us in the States – "my plane is late," "the phone didn't ring," "I missed my appointment," "I got a traffic ticket!!" proved to be insignificant little bumps in the road of life when compared to the challenges encountered in places like Nepal or Afghanistan where just getting clean water, healthy food, and planning a trip to the next village could occupy our entire day – and, by the way, you're having fun!

After Patty left, Bill spent many a night at the Chong Shop in Bodha. Chong is a Tibetan style beer and it was brewed right on the premises. Big barrels of fermenting barley and millet lined the tiny pathway through the slop to an open courtyard and primitive benches. Three stories of bricks housed many, many people living above the seething, rancid brewery. Sitting in the brewery courtyard, Bill and the other nightly denizens enjoyed a view of the mountains and the terraced rice fields below while getting thoroughly inebriated.

Bill held court nightly, post-Patty, in a bitter state of mind. He enlightened many an adventuresome tourist to the evils of Chairman Mao who, he said, used Tibetans as slaves in the deadly dangerous jobs building his huge dam projects . . . the dark side of the Nepalese monarchy . . . the evils of the British Royal family, McNamara, Kissinger, and why Jimi Hendrix was a wanker on guitar.

Tent Tom Family

English Andy

Well Fed Fred

Chapter Twenty-Eight

*"If I were a grave-digger or even a hang man, there are some
people I could work for with a great deal of enjoyment."*
DOUGLAS JERROLD 1803-1857

D ean the Dream showed up in Nepal and told us a harrowing
tale.

There was a little ice cream and coffee shop on the second
floor of a building just off Connaught Circus in New Delhi. For
many, many years, Indian intellectuals and artists had mingled
on the veranda enjoying the sweets and sharing the sacred herb.
It was an easy place for Indira Gandhi's ever more militant and

Dean the Dream

escalating state bureaucracy
in India to target. On his way
back to Kathmandu via a red-
eye, cheapo plane ticket, Bill
Wassman found himself on
the veranda with Dean the
Dream and a few other road
warriors and their female
companions. In a "round up
the usual suspects" operation,
one high-profile Indian artist,
one European couple and Bill,
representing America, were
picked out of the crowd and

arrested as arbitrary choices. Dean was somehow overlooked. It cost Bill nearly a month in the squalor of Tihar prison and then deportation to the States. It almost cost Dean the Dream his life.

Dean was staying at the Imperial Hotel, an eminent road traveler haven and a comfortable choice for the seasoned Asia veteran. He was afraid to return to his room because he thought the ice cream and coffee shop was such an obvious choice for the raid that this "flying drug squad" might swoop in on another obvious choice such as the Imperial. With just the cash he had on hand for the night, he checked into a sleazy Delhi hotel that had cubicles for rooms and a bathroom for thirty down the hall.

Unable to sleep because of the noise in the ceiling-less room that also allowed the muggy, filthy air of New Delhi to seep into his cubicle, Dean the Dream ended up in the clutches of Charles Sobhraj who happened to be wandering about near his hotel at 3:00 A.M., an hour that is always dangerous in the third world. Dean the Dream met what appeared to be at first glance a European couple. They claimed that Indian Airlines had lost their luggage and thus they were forced to try to find cheap accommodations in the middle of the night. They were both drinking from a bottle of Fanta soda and speaking in French-accented crude English. Pointing across the street, Dean the Dream told them what a horror show his own hotel was and said if they could afford anything else to find it. The European couple suggested they all go up to Dean's hotel anyway, since it was so close, and enjoy some blonde Lebanese hash that the girl had smuggled inside her body and that she was very anxious to remove.

Whether out of loneliness, boredom, or the curious sense of a man living his life on the road, Dean invited them up to his hotel. Within minutes of the three of them settling into Dean's cubicle, and in an unguarded moment, the European male hit Dean over the head with his empty Fanta bottle. Fortunately for Dean, the door to his accommodation was paper thin. The blow caused him to fall backwards, through the door, and he landed flat on his back in the middle of the hallway. It was now about 4:00 A.M., and also fortunately for Dean, a "john" was arguing over the agreed upon price with a lady of the night only two doors down. Leaving his argument for a moment, he approached the scene of the commotion. Sobhraj and his evil, female consort then dashed down the stairs and were gone.

Bill, after he got out of Tihar Prison, had to make his way back to New York City before returning to Kathmandu in order to replenish the finances that he had expended on the Indian legal system. Dean the Dream arrived in Kathmandu with tales of his misadventures in Delhi and warnings of what he felt could be a serial criminal on the hashish trail. Dean was suspicious because of the way the guy had invoked the Lebanese blonde to entice him up to the room. Sharing one form of cannabis or another was a sacramental ritual on the trail and unsuspecting travelers could easily be lured in this way. It was a few short months later, when pictures of Sobhraj in his many disguises started showing up in the international media, that Dean the Dream was able to confirm he was almost victim twenty-four in the "official" count.

Chapter Twenty-Nine

Robert, Lord Clive of India, in 1744, twice failed to shoot himself.
After the second attempt he declared:
"It appears I am destined for something. I will live."

The owner of the property we bought in California was the first Federal Forest Ranger appointed by President Franklin Roosevelt in 1933. His territory ranged from the Napa Valley to the Oregon border. "There are 10,000 paper pushers in my old territory now," he would often tell me. While surveying the land for the Forest Service he had discovered the waterfalls and bought the land. Once he did, using federal bulldozers, he cut a firebreak out to a perfect homesite. He retired there in 1963 after 30 years of duty to the Forest Service.

Centuries before, Mt. Lassen had been an active volcano and Dirty Creek, cutting through the lava, had left a wonderful grotto. Developing the place into an organic paradise became a labor of love. Skipper Gary built an authentic sauna that allowed one to toast at 190 degrees and then leap into the cool, clear creek.

We improved the existing garden by creating bio-dynamic, raised beds. The orchard was expanded with additional fruit and nut trees. We built a first-class, four-box stall, horse barn. Sure-footed Appaloosas, perfect for the rough terrain, were the horse of choice. Tent Tom created a unique Tibetan tent for the garden. Along with the Tibetan snow leopards and lotus flowers, the tent must have had appliqués of fertility symbols because, over time,

two earth mothers conceived within those canvas walls.

A couple of guys talked me into growing marijuana commercially. I agreed to their proposal for botanical knowledge, and because I wanted to see and enjoy the results produced by my collection of imported seeds.

High-end imported grass was valued at four times the price of "California Homegrown." Homegrown was considered second-rate to the plants cultivated on the slopes of the Andes, the jungles of Jamaica or the verdant highlands of Thailand. Our slogan was: "with good seeds, nine months of care and careful cultivation under full sun, plenty of water, and organically enriched soil, even an idiot can come up with something just as tasty."

Our crop had the advantage of enjoying a true southern exposed slope into which the bio-dynamic beds were carved.

Every bit of soil was sifted through screens to remove even the smallest pebble and mixed with manure and free-range chicken poop to create a fluffy plot. The hard part was being scratched by the manzanita, eaten by the mosquitoes, and caked with mud spatter while tending the plants.

At harvest time, my two partners said, "This stuff is so good we're going to get twice as much money as any home-grown!"

The mother of invention is also inspired by unrelenting mosquito bites. Thus my idea: include one T-shirt with each ounce sold at a price equal to that of the imported weed. The first T-shirt was a very direct sales pitch. It was emblazoned with the word "Sensamil-

Illustration by Bird-in-the-Hand

UNCOMMON SENSE

Until taught by pain...
mankind knows not what
water is worth... Byron

John Stanton in his college football jersey
was the model for this illustration

lia" [sic] written across the front and "Sweet, Virgin, Spicy" underneath an image of a beautiful young girl with stars in her eyes, rainbows around her head and bud spilling out of the basket she was carrying. At first the market said, "It's too much for 'home-grown' but if I get one of those T-shirts I'll take it this time!"

After that initial sampling it was "more, more, may I have another T-shirt, please?" By the second season, people were asking equally for the T-shirt and the herb.

Homegrown became a growth industry for the impoverished lumber community. People showed up like the Forty-niners who had originally settled this part of California and started growing. I watched them literally buying land, living in a tent, growing weed, building a cabin, another growing season, putting in a water system and toilet, another successful year, building a barn and sauna, growing weed and getting a new truck. In between there'd often be a baby or two.

The nearby town benefited as well. A Little League field was built, equipment was upgraded for the local volunteer fire department and a little fairground was cleared for an annual summer festival. It was truly a golden time for back-to-the-earth folks desiring a green lifestyle. Anywhere from six to thirty-six people hung out in the swimming holes at any time. Kachook also had a girlfriend; a female dog that was brought to our ranch by a couple of other Asia refugees from tribal Pakistan. She was named Oman Neeka. This beautiful bitch became Kachook's mate and they had two litters together.

Geese roamed the gardens; the chickens free ranged and lived in a pyramid-shaped chicken coop built on the exact model of the Egyptian pyramids just to see if the eggs would come out more nutritious . . . or square.

I pushed the belief that, like the ever growing wine industry of California now making big money for families whose grandfathers had done jail time during Prohibition, our children would similarly benefit when sanity prevailed politically and cannabis was legal.

A deputy sheriff had policed this area for more than thirty years. His main problems were stolen car choppers. The thieves would bring a car up into the dense woods, strip it and leave the remains. If they got away with it once, they came back up a second time. He also had to deal with deer poachers who were incredibly dangerous. Most of them were abjectly poor folks, often from other Northern California counties, who had been arrested numerous times for poaching deer and were facing serious jail time for repeated offenses. They were armed to the teeth and ready to draw down. Everyone in the area respected the deputy for working solo and taking on these desperadoes.

The deputy stopped by the ranch once in awhile for coffee. He, like most people, was fond of Rebecca and would often say to me, "To protect your wife from one of these lowlifes, if anyone comes up here and gives you any trouble, just hit 'em right through the windshield and call me. I'll take care of it from there."

Chapter Thirty

"The Lama said on my deathbed I'd receive total enlightenment . . . so I've got that going for me."

BILL MURRAY AS CARL SPACKLER IN THE MOVIE *"CADDY SHACK"*

Another winter approached and Rebecca and I went back to Nepal. Our itinerary included a slow, steady, pace with studious, serious field trips, at times picking up a treasure or two here and there. We were weaving our way through the haze of clove cigarettes in Java, the pools of red betel nut spit on the sidewalks of India and Indonesia, or the stench from cigars constantly smoked by both sexes in Northern Thailand; then finally wending our way over to Kathmandu to oversee the expanding Tibetan carpet business.

Wassman and I rode Russian motorcycles. They were a perfect copy of the great American-made Triumph Bonneville. The Russian bikes had big, fancy gas tanks. They never started on the first kick and could just reach the speed limit. But, as Bill said, "It was a very sexy looking machine." Wassman would putt-putt around with a Dharma-ite behind him. "Dharma-ites" were what we called the girls who had come to the east to absorb some Buddhism.

Ted claimed that since infancy he had never been on a motorcycle other than a BMW. Cathy was currently refusing to ride with him because of a couple of run-ins with errant water buffalo or meandering rickshaws, which she blamed on his constant state of mild inebriation. She drove a moped.

Bill told the Dharma-ites that his wife had left him after tiring of being forced to survive like the poorest Sadhu in southern India. One evening, Bill told us that things had come to a culmination point for him and Patty when a rich Indian, after a late night drunken debacle, had actually pulled a gun and demanded sex with Patty. Fortunately, the maniac had drunk himself into a stupor so that they could escape at three or four in the morning. When Bill flagged down a car outside the villa and the driver offered to take them to the next town, Bill refused because the driver's price was too high. Luckily, they survived, but this was the last straw for Patty.

Things seemed to have come full circle, as many of these new arrivals were wearing the silk harem pants that Rebecca and I had produced in Asia and sent to Frankfurt. "Dharma-ites, wearing clothes made of silk brocade from China, tailored in Afghanistan and sold in Europe, are riding on the back seat of a Russian motorcycle driven by an obsessed American in Nepal," quipped Cathy about her friend Bill. "It's a small world."

Tantric sex was also in the gestalt of the new female Dharma-ites. Bill had experimented with Tantra during his marriage and easily became comfortable as an appreciative mentor. Tantric sex requires discipline and practice – Rebecca and I found it enjoyable, if rather taxing, preferring a more spontaneous, romantic approach.

Business-wise, life was not so pleasant. I had a growing problem with the new Tibetan mafia that had recently come into being in Nepal.

The Tibetan mafia was not a violent or criminal organization in the Western sense. They had the power to control dyes and export quotas. The mafia kept the "nouveau riche" Tibetans in line through gambling and drinking. Each major holiday found more and more workers enslaved for their future carpet profits because of drunken gambling losses.

The mafia could not affect my business directly because I used Yak wool and natural dyes. Nor could the Tibetan mafia control my little "designer niche" Walloon carpets because they came in from Bhutan where the Walloon clan was thriving in that sanctuary. As far at the Tibetan Tiger carpets, the energetic Thamal traders were only too happy to search them out for top dollar. But my Nepalese customs broker and shipping company could be intimidated. They would shrug and say they could not ship on the days promised or even ship at all!

At the same time, the temple thieves and museum rip-offs were doing very nicely, thank you. So, I put together a big, one-of-a-kind museum-quality, probably stolen, antique sale, partnering up with Well Fed Fred. The former Hog Farmer was well entrenched in the Kathmandu Valley, and, like everyone else who wanted to stay there, was trying to market Tibetan carpets, find an antique to sell, or smuggle hash. In this instance, Well Fed Fred had stumbled upon an extremely wealthy European collector. He had already managed to pull off a $20,000 deal with the gentleman.

My contribution to the deal was a 1000-year-old Jain statue that I obtained with the help of a Nepali antiquities specialist. It was a religious object known as a Pathfinder. The Pathfinder was sculpted in an era when the Jain religion was at its height. The statue had made its way to Nepal after having been stolen from an Indian museum by one of the museum's custodial employees, and spirited to Kathmandu. Well Fed had the connection who was willing to pay cash money with no questions asked. We flew to Europe with statue in hand.

Everything about this particular expedition was difficult at first because I got off the plane at Amsterdam's Schiphol Airport with a mild case of flu. Well Fed Fred rented a car at the airport. We embarked upon a smorgasbord of destinations in Europe from Belgium to Cologne to Düsseldorf as Fred tried second, third and fourth attempts to sell the statue for more than the original deal. While I moaned, complained and held on for dear life in the back seat, Well Fed feasted on the local cuisine consisting of pickled herring, potato frites with mayonnaise, and mountain oyster stew followed by a hardy stein or two of dark ale, all of which, of course, producing prodigious amounts of flatulence.

We finally arrived at our intended destination and sold the Pathfinder for five figures in five minutes to the original buyer.

Mr. Big Time Collector spoke excellent English and held a special passion for religious artifacts. Russian Orthodox icons adorned one wall of the drawing room of his house that was located in a charming, bourgeois European neighborhood. At one point during the tour of his treasures he asked, "Do you boys know that the Dalai Lama is here tonight giving a talk?" We admitted we didn't. He chided us a bit saying, "You're both supposedly Kathmandu aficionados and should know that this is the Dalai Lama's momentous first trip to Europe." He demonstrated his expertise by a wave of his arm in the direction of another wall of rare, Tibetan spiritual artifacts and *tankas*. He then invited us to attend the talk.

Cash in the pocket always seems to makes a bit of illness more tolerable. Nonetheless I remember very little of the occasion apart from the dark wood of the interior. A feeling of traditional academic custom and pomp permeated the small auditorium where the address took place. Fortunately, we were brought through the receiving line, and when both Well Fed Fred and I were able to say our greetings and a couple of other phrases in basic Tibetan, His Holiness was very pleased. We explained that we had just arrived from Kathmandu and he asked us a question about life in Nepal. Well Fed answered in Tibetan for both of us. His Holiness smiled warmly and bowed as we were ushered along. There was something about the easy exchange of pleasantries with this simple monk that made me feel lighter than air for days. After Well Fed showed everyone in the Katmandu Valley a photo of us with His Holiness and gushed about our spiritual fortune, a more practical benefit occurred. The Tibetan mafia left me alone.

Chapter Thirty-One

"We can't all be heroes because somebody has to sit on the curb
and clap as they go by."

WILL ROGERS

One winter we went down to Puerto Vallarta, Mexico. Dean the Dream was throwing a weeklong bash to celebrate his success at jumping an invisible line that is the border between countries. Dean had rented "Los Areoboles," which translated to "the Grandfather's house." It was a luxurious Mediterranean villa complete with indoor/outdoor pool and waterfall grotto, bathing suit bar and grand views of the Pacific Ocean.

Most of that's not for me, so I started playing in a two-man volleyball game. The games were held on the beach in front of a four-star hotel for the interest of twenty to thirty guests. Each team put up some pesos . . . winner take all with a tip for the net judge. This volleyball game would lead Rebecca and me toward spending a little bit of time around Bob Dylan in Yalapa.

We went out to Yalapa with Manny Shapiro, whom I met around the volleyball courts in PV. Manny promoted the Beatles show at the Hollywood Bowl, as well as the Doors and other big name acts. He had gotten into tax trouble with Uncle Sam and had to move to Mexico. He now promoted shows such as The Commodores and Earth, Wind and Fire in Mexico City and Guadalajara. A sophisticated gentleman and excellent promoter, he made a good peso. He had a big villa in Yalapa, a small village on the bay at the tip of a peninsula. It took three hours to get there by boat. The rugged jungle terrain was impossible to build a road through, thus safeguarding the pristine area from casual tourism. Yalapa was technically under a treaty the Mexican government had signed with seven different Indian tribes whose lands encompassed the peninsula. The corrupt and feared Mexican police, known as "Federales," had no jurisdiction there. This was a comforting thought and thus a small community of artists and pot smokers had integrated itself into the indigenous populace.

Manny bet on my volleyball partner, Stormin' Norman, and me. Norman was a collegiate, scholarship player and I'd been playing since childhood and had a decent game. Even though we weren't good enough to win the tournament at first, we did develop teamwork and started winning more and more games each day.

The sand in front of the beach resort was peppercorn. Peppercorn grains of sand are particularly big and abrasive. After a week of pure sport, Stormin' Norman and I played two hot shots from Santa Cruz. We held our own in a heated, competitive contest, primarily because our feet had grown leather-like after a gradual buildup of protective callous. By the time we won the tortuous, marathon contest, the superior talent, new to Puerto Vallarta and that peppercorn sand, were torn up and bleeding.

Manny, happy with his long-shot winnings, invited Rebecca and me to visit his villa on Yalapa. He cajoled me to "get out there and rent a house" because, as he put it, "There are a couple of special guests coming that are your age." Manny said he "needed some young company." Manny had young children of his own, conceived late in life, and no adult kids. These two "special guests" were Bob Dylan and Dennis Hopper. We took his advice and found a charming little beachside bungalow.

Bob Dylan had just finished his "Rolling Thunder" tour. On that tour, Dylan brought in different people to play at the different venues. People rolled in for a few days and then out, in an ever-changing cast of musicians, celebrities, and artists. Dylan, who was invited for post-tour rest at Manny's villa, showed up accompanied by Hopper and Jim Franklin. Franklin had been with the tour on the final gig. He was an artist from Texas known for incorporating armadillos in his Americana pastels of Texas landscapes. He also created the artwork for a calendar commissioned by Justin Boots – the famous Texas cowboy boot manufacturer. I had crossed paths with Franklin when he was hand-drawing the three armadillos on the paper wrapping that covered kilos of Mexican grass for a brand known as "Tres Armadillos." The Shapiro family had an old friendship with Dennis Hopper from their mutual Hollywood roots. Hopper was a counter-culture hero of mine, because of his self-made success in a movie industry fraught with nepotism.

The next night Manny's wife, May, arranged for all of us to go to a local shaman healing ceremony. The ceremony was performed on the grounds of a house owned by a full-time resident American couple who had gone to great lengths to make it a special occasion. After the ceremony, Rebecca and I met the hosts. We found that they were deeply immersed in the local tribal spirituality, frequently using peyote in their rituals. They were operating their lives under the belief system that Yalapa was a special place and that it had been "chosen" as a landing site to receive UFO emissaries.

Every moment I was around Dennis Hopper I was stupefied. I was possessed by an overwhelming desire to ask him what kind of mission his father was on during World War II when his family was informed he had been killed. Why would his wife and child need to believe that? Hooper's mother had remarried, then one day in 1946, Dennis Hooper opened the door and saw his father, believed dead for three years! I was obsessed with trying to delicately broach that subject. What kind of mission could be that secret? Was it behind enemy lines? A double agent? So cognizant of trying to find the right way and right time, I never said a word.

Yalapa beach was a about a kilometer long and crescent shaped. At one end was a small palapa hammock-style hotel and at the other a cliff that overlooked the bay and required quite a walk up a goat trail to get home. The locals and gringos all had to traverse the path. It kept the scene small. The daily arrival and departure of the Puerto Vallarta ferryboat was the only activity in that quiet, languid paradise. Dylan found a shady spot and sketched the scenery most days.

Dennis Hopper rousted up the beach crowd to play ten-on-a-side mad-cap volleyball. He even induced Dylan to join in on a couple of occasions. Rebecca was an eager participant and played on Dylan's team one day and Hopper's the next. Hopper always played with a bottle of beer or Jack Daniels in one hand. I watched one of the games with Jim Franklin. He was very excited because Dylan had commissioned him to paint an armadillo mural on the bottom of his swimming pool at his new home in Point Dune.

The special memorable highlight of those weeks was hearing Dylan perform the songs from his "Desire" album, acoustically. He came strolling down the beach at sunset carrying his guitar and singing to himself. Then he mumbled to the crowd assembled in front of the Hammock Hotel, waiting for the green flash, that he was going to celebrate the release of his album in the U.S. that very day by revisiting some of the songs. It was a musical experience to rival any, ever. He delivered "Isis," "Sarah," and "Mozambique," with a magical beach party feeling. The ballad about Ruben "Hurricane" Carter was incredible, engaging and forceful in capturing the feeling and empathy generated by a wronged man "who is in a prison cell but at one time he coulda been the champion of the world." Bob Dylan's performance of "Hurricane," delivered barefoot and microphone-free in the tropical twilight, surely matched any impassioned plea for justice ever sung: "I just as soon go on my way, up to some paradise where the trout stream flows and the air is nice, and ride a horse along a trail," brings tears to my eyes.

The spell was broken when Hopper came into the circle with his arms around two good-looking girls shouting "Heavy metal, heavy metal! Hey Bob, will you do 'Stairway to Heaven'?"

Chapter Thirty-Two

*Asked how he could play so well when he was loaded? Zoot Sims
said . . . "I practiced when I was loaded."*

QUOTED IN JAZZ ANECDOTES

It's always good to return home. A rhythm had been established;
we enjoyed the ranch, gardening, riding the Appaloosas, birth-
ing the pups, yoga and swimming. There was an endless flow of
like minds, friends and neighbors. In the winter it was back to
work. One-of-a-kind, museum-quality treasures were in great demand. The Tibetan carpets were selling steadily.

I was also doing very well, financially, by promoting, silent-
partnering, or producing musical shows for the local college crowd.
The state university had, at that time, about 8,000 party-hungry
students. Each show was a sure thing as long as you were in tune
with the current musical desires. Groups that were popular, such
as Fleetwood Mac, Santana and Taj Mahal, came through town
on their coastal swings to or from San Francisco. The booking
contracts of that era allowed a promoter to prohibit a band from
performing for two weeks within the area on either side of their
gig. Bill Graham, the renowned, powerful booking agent from San
Francisco, insisted on this provision. Fortunately that contract
contained a clause that limited his control to a radius of 150 miles.
The college was 157 miles from San Francisco. The clause provided
a spot for groups that needed a night between their San Francisco
gig and their next show to or from Oregon or Washington.

In the mid-seventies reggae music hit. It was love at first sight and sound, especially the shank guitar and bubble keyboard parts incorporated in the unrelenting dance beat. Within two weeks of seeing Bob Marley with some 400 other people at the Boarding House in San Francisco, Rebecca and I were on a plane to Jamaica.

With great disappointment, it quickly became apparent that Jamaica was not the palm tree and sandy beach island paradise of my imagination. The aluminum bauxite mines and industrial base had created an island ruled by violent politics, labor bosses and gangsters. The musician's union was all powerful. The only reggae you could hear on the island was played by cover bands in tourist hotels. Bob Marley rarely performed on the island of Jamaica.

It was during this pioneering foray into the reggae world that a trip down to Trench Town to score some weed led to a meeting with some members of a local band called Culture. In Trench Town the guys from Culture informed me that you could hear real reggae music performed at Jump Ups on St. Vincent, or Bequia, in the Grenadine Islands. They said they were going to be playing a Jump Up on Bequia soon.

Down in Trench Town, a guy would sit cross-legged on a tenement stoop with a basket of swamp weed on one side, a roll of aluminum foil between his legs and another basket on the other side. He would grab a pinch of weed from one basket, roll it in the tin foil, quickly twist the two ends and throw it into another basket – poetry in motion! Since money was so tight, Jamaicans bought these "Jamaican Bullets" for a dollar, one "bullet" at a time.

The Caribbean was not the only place where "bullet" was the slang for packaging a small amount of cannabis. When Rebecca and I were in the Lankowi Islands, a small group of islands off the coast of Malaysia, we were given the following instructions through the traveler's grapevine regarding how to score a bit of the herb: "Go to the bank, the owner's lazy son will be sitting at a desk all by himself and bored to tears. Offer to rent his Honda 90

motorcycle. Money will do him no good, being the son of the rich-
est guy on the island with nothing to spend it on; however, for a
couple of rock and roll cassettes he will rent his motorcycle for a
day. Drive to the fish market in Poco Assam."

I walked into the bank as instructed – there was a guy at a
desk and he was half asleep, it had to be the banker's son. We cut
a deal for a Rolling Stones and Led Zeppelin cassettes and headed
out on the motorcycle to Poco Assam.

My instructions had been to go to the fish market and just
stand around. "Don't worry," I was told, "Just when you think
that no one is going to pay any attention to you, a teenager will
come over and give you a nod. Follow him." And follow him we did,
back into some of the thickest mangrove on earth, tunneled out
until it opened up into a space where cardboard was spread on the
sand and bamboo bongs hung from the branches. Just across the
strait, within sight, was the island of Sumatra. Sumatra is famous
for white tigers, coffee, and for growing some of the finest golden
herb on the planet. In Poco Assam this golden Sumatran weed
was wrapped in tin foil and sold individually, just as in Jamaica,
and known as "bullets." I was assured by the local tokers that it
was only every couple of months that the police came. Even then
they merely took the cardboard and broke up the bamboo bongs.
Nonetheless, we bought up all we could and, complying with my
all-encompassing rule to "get the herb and get out," we hopped
back on the Honda 90 and got the hell out of there.

On the advice of the muscians in Culture, we flew to the island of St. Vincent, the capital of the Grenadine chain, where we
hoped to find true reggae music. St. Vincent proved to be another
island plagued by politics, pills and pistols. A wealthy enclave
was the departure point for people going on seven-day cruises
through the islands either on rented yachts or private sailboats.
Each major island to the south was a pleasant four- to eight-hour
sail. It was also possible to get on a mail boat for one night only.
The great discovery was a working sailing vessel, "The Friendship

Rose," that took cargo and people twice weekly to Bequia. Bequia was where those who made a living from the "cruising" lived; the sailboat captains, cooks and crews. Jump Ups were held there twice a week. Weed was plentiful and the group, Culture, performed. We rented a house for a month at five bucks a day on the windward side in La Pumpas. La Pumpas was the last whaling village left in the Caribbean. Daily we jogged, swam and ate exotic culinary delights of the sea. Two or three nights a week Culture would lay down a rhythm that drove one to move and dance. The road manager of the group improved the attitude of all with "magic Jamaican bullets."

I got to know the main players in Culture and made arrangements to go back quickly to St. Vincent's only recording studio and produce a song. Their song "International Herb" was way cool and needed to be heard. A side note that came out of this session was on one of the song's ride outs. The singer threw in a few places in the world where ganja was grown. However, if you listen to the ride out closely, you will hear places named where ganja isn't found; those being Taiwan and Bermuda.

Part of the lure of traveling is leaving yourself open to unanticipated, unplanned experiences. This time I was approached by a sprightly 85-year-old captain who pointed to his beautiful 100 ft. sailboat anchored off my favorite exercise beach on Bequia. "I see you on the beach, frequently with your wife? I was wondering if you would like to sail with me and my wife over to Mustique?" I gladly accepted.

His wife was a lovely "thirty-something" woman from Nova Scotia. Our host had served in the Coast Guard earlier in his life for 55 years and retired to his boat. The secret to his vital longevity, he assured us, was that he ate only one meal of bouillabaisse every day while in the Coast Guard pre-World War II. He said "That's all they fed us." He and Eve had been married two years and they were the ones who ferried Mick Jagger, his wife Bianca and their young daughter, Jade, back and forth from Bequia to

Mustique when the Jagger family visited their estate on the secluded island. "Pays good for an Englishman," the captain added.

Princess Margaret also had an estate there. One of the reasons Mustique was a playground for the ultra rich only was that it has no rainfall. 99.9% of all water has to be imported at great expense.

The boat was greeted quite warmly at Basil's Restaurant and Yacht Club. The captain commandeered a jeep and we drove right up to the Cliffside estates. Eve showed us around the vacant Jagger home. It was while viewing Princess Margaret's grounds that the realization hit me – acres of lawns were being doused with water costing $100.00 a gallon.

We moved down the Grenadines chain from yacht to yacht by invitation. We once obtained passage on a mail-carrying boat. We spent a night on Petit St. Vincent, also a destination stop of the very wealthy. It's a tiny island that accommodates 22 people maximum. At the far end of the chain is Grenada. What is etched in my memory is that an American navel ship arrived while we were there. Jimmy Carter was President at the time and a naval fleet on a good will mission came to the island. A group of U.S. sailors/musicians played spirited cover versions of classic rock and roll songs, much to the delight of the locals. A few years later, this very same island was invaded by American forces under the pretense of stopping some sort of ridiculous Cuban military action. The Cubans were actually building a tourist airstrip and had no guns. Three hundred and thirty-one American boys were killed by "friendly fire." I believe that showing up with a horn section could have saved those lives.

Our last free ride was on a yacht over to the islands of Martinique and Guadaloupe; the two French provinces in the Caribbean. The interesting thing here is that we finished the trip at an incredibly unique French plantation "de La Ritz," where we stayed inexpensively. It was located at 2,500 ft. and it was still a working banana plantation. We were served two fabulous French meals daily and given horses to ride. The views were spectacular from the dormant volcano's altitude. We enjoyed tennis on the lawn courts as well as swimming in a gigantic, fresh water pool. The freshwater was piped in directly from a spring a thousand feet higher on the mountainside and the spray rose 40 ft. in the air before it fed the pool. For brain food, the plantation offered a treasure trove of historical documents and maps from the late 1700s.

The noted European photographer, Uli Rose, and his wife Honey were the only other guests at the plantation. Honey had been the first black woman to appear in a Maidenform bra ad. They'd met and married through the fashion work. Uli had just finished shooting a swimsuit issue for a sports magazine and they were enjoying a little rest and relaxation.

Then there was Martin Blinder. Blinder gained notoriety for being the expert witness who came up with what is known as the "Twinkie defense" in the infamous Dan White trial. White had murdered Harvey Milk and the Mayor of San Francisco, George Moscone. Blinder had given expert testimony that White lived on soft drinks, candy bars and Hostess Twinkies snacks, which affected him such that he could not be held responsible for his actions. Blinder's analysis and testimony was considered largely responsible for getting White only four years for those two murders. Blinder was using his sizeable fee to celebrate with someone he called "Sex Monkey." We never learned any other name because Blinder called her only that. She said proudly that the nickname was based on a character in a Philip Roth novel.

Chapter Thirty-Three

Atman: a man who has entered into a mystical state wherein he has thrown off his ego; a man who has realized his greater self; a man, who, through a process of realization of his true nature as a human, identifies himself with, and so becomes, universal spirit.
In Hinduism and Buddhism: a seer.

ASIA

O n one of our Asian visits, Rebecca had a little bout of dysentery and stayed at the Imperial Hotel while I went to a dusty, bureaucratic office in New Delhi to try to obtain the necessary paperwork to go to the tiny Himalayan kingdom of Sikkim. Sikkim was home to the Karmapa, the father of Karma, and one of the four pillars of Buddhist thought. I had heard that the Karmapa annually performed the Black Hat Ceremony in which he transforms himself from a human being into a lion for those in attendance. I wanted to be there.

The Kingdom of Sikkim had been governed by a Chogyal. In 1963 an American woman named Hope Cooke married the Chogyal of Sikkim and eventually bore him two children. Indira Gandhi, in a show of strength to her military commanders, had swallowed up the tiny kingdom by invading it. Gandhi had been able to do so with minor resistance because the Chogyal's wife had become so unpopular with the populace. Hope generally conducted her affairs like a girl in the Peace Corps and her behavior had broken the majesty and grandeur associated with the power of a centuries-old political system.

I spent an hour in the dusty office and no one said a word to me. In fact, the Indian official did not say anything to anyone. I did some verbal prodding – to no avail.

Unbeknownst to me at the time, the invasion of Sikkim by India was underway and the abdication by the Chogyal and his family had taken place. The Indian bureaucrats, it seemed, were making it difficult for anyone to visit. I was ready to give up.

In that office a small, wizened man leaned on a cane and was being supported by two Buddhist monks. When they were refused permission to return to their monastery in Sikkim, I had my first clue to the invasion. The old man, bent and hunched, shuffled away supported by the monks. As he pased me he stopped and said, "I am the Atman and I've been waiting for you. Follow me."

The summons was almost hypnotic and rather compelling, so I did. They hailed an open-air taxi, a tuk-tuk, and we were taken to a nearby ashram where he and the two monks were staying.

The Atman had studied under the Karmapa in Sikkim for most of his adult life and that evening it wasn't long before I found myself in a ritual of incense, hypnosis and energy control that was an epiphany and revelation of mental possibilities. The Atman practiced the transformation techniques that he had learned from the Karmapa on me.

He took me to a small, unadorned room at the ashram. He placed, with great ceremony, a assortment of substances into a charcoal fire, one at a time. These ingredients were then mixed with a variety of herbs and incense. Breathing this blend resulted in an opening of the channels of the brain and a hallucinatory experience. The Atman then began a lecture that compared the various religions of the world. Just as his teacher, the Karmapa, transformed himself into a lion to get the attention of his students, the Atman was able to transform himself. This creaky old man, who could barely walk without the support of two young monks, became a sprightly Irish Catholic divinity student, complete with brogue, as he imparted information on Christianity. When he spoke of Islam and its great truths, the Atman became a Bedouin in the desert complete with a sirocco wind. Explaining Buddhism, the Atman transformed himself into Milarepa, the colorful poet and troubadour of that philosophy. He finished by telling me five things that would become true in the next year. Only if and when they became true, should I visit him in a Buddhist monastery in Penang, Malaysia.

The five things were:

1) I would rid myself of anything but total consciousness and awareness of everyday details of life. For example, no more searching for temporarily misplaced keys;

2) I would never smoke tobacco again, because tobacco addicts pass on the addiction to their children;

3) I would joyously receive an unexpected financial gain;

4) An artist that I knew would move to the next dimension from this body early in his life;

5) A meditation house would be built on some magical land I lived on.

The only thing the Atman knew about me was that I was an American. He did not know my living circumstances or even my name when he told me the five predictions.

My use of tobacco was sparse and so I found it was easy to eliminate it in a short while. His psychological imprint on my consciousness relieved the anxiety I normally experienced looking for things like lost keys and I made that improvement.

Jelly Roll Troy, one of the great bass players and a friend, passed on before he was 30. The news was shocking. His life had been that of a star-crossed artist who, at age fourteen, started out on the biggest rock and roll tour a musician could play and ended his career with the most money he'd ever made from music in his pocket when he checked into the hospital for his final days. That check was for his work on the soundtrack of a porno movie. Because it was porno, Mike Bloomfield had accepted the gig only so his musicians could have a big payday.

During that same year I had an unexpected, lucky run up to five figures when the dice got hot in Reno.

Another of the Atman's predictions came true within months when a local building contractor, who thoroughly enjoyed the ranch's sacred herb, offered to build a second home on the ranch with payment from the next harvest. He brought in his crew and created a beautiful one-bedroom cabin with a view of the canyon's waterfalls and grotto. With the completion of this meditation house, fulfilling the five prophesies, we began preparations to see the Atman again.

Chapter Thirty-Four

During a military battle with U.S., British and other European forces in Lebanon, Syrian General Mustafa Tlass instructed his men not to attack the Italian contingent of soldiers because he had a life-long obsession with the Italian movie star Gina Lollobrigida. General Tlass told his men not to attack the Italian soldiers because "I do not want a single tear falling from the eyes of Gina Lollobrigida."

With a year's reflection, I came to understand the experience I had gone through. Rebecca was eager to meet the man with these shamanistic powers so we set out to find the Atman in a Buddhist monastery on Penang Island, Malaysia.

In Penang, Indians were at the bottom of the social pecking order and hated as much as the Chinese. Most Indians were rickshaw drivers or engaged in illegal activities in order to survive, thus a source of herb. We got a hotel in the Indian quarter.

Atman

The rickshaw driver and cannabis connection was a Hindu. Atman is also recognized by the Hindu religion, overlapping with Buddhist philosophy in the belief that a human being can become a seer through spiritual techniques. The rickshaw driver sent word to the monastary that a Western couple was trying to find the Atman.

The Atman sent for us. The Buddhist temple he was staying at was incredibly ornate, stretching across a span of hillside in rural Penang.

During WWI, Japanese troops were bivoucked in the monastery. The young, superstitious, Japanese soldiers stayed away from the old Chinese cemetery on the grounds. The monks had been driven out to work in the fields for the war effort. One of the monks hid from the occupiers, in the highlands above the cemetery, and managed to sneak down and be maintained by local villagers who, at great risk, supplied him with his basic needs.

The monk's biggest difficulty was finding water. One day he moved a rock on the hillside and out gushed a fantastic stream of pure, fresh spring water. This natural spring is central to the new temple complex and fills a good-sized pool. After the war, donations poured in to create the Chinese-influenced spires and beautiful lotus-based architecture dedicated to this sacred water source.

Rebecca and I had an audience with the Atman daily, but the Atman never veered off into any mystical moments. He concentrated on things such as the importance of a vegetarian diet, the value of marriage and the need for the discipline of finding a moment for isolation and meditation in daily life.

Before we left he insisted that we make it a life goal to see the Hemis Festival in Ladakh. The Hemis Festival is the oldest continuous celebration on the planet – 2500 years old. Hemis is the stupa where the Bon, an animist, spirit worshipping sect, agreed that the Buddha's way was the superior way and accepted Buddhism. The Atman's final words were, "I will be in Sri Lanka, in the town of Kandy, where the tooth of the Buddha is held in the scared stupa Dalada Maligawa. I'll see you there next year – be ready."

As we were leaving, he added, as if it were a casual aside, "Also, Rebecca will never conceive a child."

Chapter Thirty-Five

"The use of traveling is to regulate imagination by reality, and instead of thinking how things may be, to see them as they are."

SAMUEL JOHNSON

W e started for the island of Java, the political center and the most modern of the many islands that constitute the state of Indonesia. We abandoned the capital, Jakarta, quickly. It's a horrible, smog-ridden metropolis overburdened with humanity and vehicles.

We took a train to the city of Bandung, the durian capital of the world. Durian is the foulest-smelling fruit on the planet. The city reeked of the stuff. Thankfully, we were on our way to one of the greatest beaches on the planet. Pangandaran is at the eastern coast of Java, at the end of a 22-km peninsula. The end of the peninsula is 1 km in width and is connected to a knob of land that is surrounded by 200-foot sheer cliffs. This makes it a mega-wild zoo and it was the first wildlife preserve created when the new nation of Indonesia became independent of Dutch colonial rule at the end of World War II.

What made Pangandaran so great was that people were glad to see you. It was a virgin bodysurfing spot, with immediate access to a fabulous jungle and what were called "man" trees, or platforms, built to blend into scenery and conveniently placed overlooking waterholes to observe the wildlife. We were able to observe a number of particularly fascinating species of monkeys as well as wild Cape buffalos. Another unique feature of Pangandaran was the nightly migration of giant bats, which flew out of their cave rooks and into the jungle to feed at night.

Beyond all the beauty, there was a feeling of dread that overwhelmed the pleasant experience in Pangandaran for travelers, few though they were. This fear was of the true horror of the transportation experience necessary to get to Pangandaran. One needed to cross three small coastal jungle mountain ranges in a nine-passenger vehicle, for which the operator sold 15 seats. I had to buy two extra seats just for our luggage. Still, we were squashed in. Worse was that the driver drove just as fast as he could possibly go, blasting at 120 kph across 4,000 ft. gorges over one-lane bamboo bridges. A lot of bridges and hair pin turns on a long, four-hour ride. Up and down twisting mountain roads we went, while the driver insanely drove to the max, blasting Indonesian pop music at full volume.

Each traveler we met told us of their terrible mental state at the thought of having to face the harrowing, death-defying ride out. Rebecca vowed not to leave until we found another way. In so doing, we had one of the most fortunate experiences a traveler can fall into.

We discovered that once a month a mail boat departed from a port 19 km away. It was an integral and vital source of transportation for the locals and served as their primary means of transportation to the next big city, which was Chilliachop. We jumped at the opportunity and booked passage on the next mail boat from this small, minor port along the coast. From there, we took a horse taxi for six km to another nine-passenger "bemo-hub." From there it was mercifully only a half-hour to a railhead where we grabbed a train into Jag Jakarta.

The mail boat ride out was full of surprises. We stopped at small, indigenous fishing villages where the inhabitants paddled out to the mail boat in colorful canoes to get provisions and a bag of mail – this was their only link to modern civilization. Every so often, we would chug around a bend and be treated to a scattering flock of incredibly beautiful and colorful jungle birds or an exotic family of wild animals on the shore taking a drink of water.

Jag Jakarta was Java's capital before it became part of Indonesia and it proved to be a wonderful place. It is the home of the great Buddhist stupa, Borobudur – a replica of the cosmos, symbolizing the ten levels of a Bodhisattva's life which must be developed to become a Buddha or an awakened one.

Jag Jakarta hosted a wonderful museum that gave a cultural overlay to the island's history. Jag Ja, as it was affectionately known by travelers, was also home to a fabulous cuisine. One favorite was an omelet-like dish prepared on the spot by street chefs, while another culinary delight was a steamed rice dish served out of a bamboo holder drizzled through with hot cane sugar.

There was a traveler's hotel, which meant mosquito nets and fans, plus no rattling, dripping, and disease-causing second-rate air-conditioning unit. Borobudur, the great museum, and the healthy, tasty food attracted the best kind of international crowd. We enjoyed intellectual and philosophical exchanges in the elaborate garden of the hotel, where you could catch a fragrant breeze and some sun, and exchange a little chunk of Kashmiri hash for a bit of Thai bud.

Next on the agenda was a trip to one of the end-of-the-world surf sites – Parentrides. It started with a bus trip south on a road that ended at a river. Because surfers desired the waves Parentrides offered, a ferry business had come into being. Trolls and outcasts, who previously were barely able to exist along the river's edge, had now established profitable businesses taking advantage of the influx of visitors. When we got to the opposite side of the river, we climbed up and over a one-mile sand dune. Surprisingly, as soon as we reached the other side of the sand dune we were met by half a dozen adolescent girls selling ice cream cone-shaped paper cups full of psychedelic mushrooms. Everybody, at all times in Parentrides, was high on "shrooms," especially some really tough and talented Aussie surfers.

Most surfers were on odysseys, surf pilgrimages actually, to hit all the beaches on Java's coasts. The waters boiled in this bay. I wouldn't go in knee deep and neither would anybody who grew up there. The locals fished only for minnows close to the shore. Other daring residents eked out a living by climbing the vines up the sea cliffs to harvest the nests that were a key ingredient for the birds nest soup sold to diners in Hong Kong as a delicacy.

After a couple of days of trying to survive on minnow soup and boiled roots it was back over that one-mile dune and out. We had to pay the snapping, surly trolls who ran the ferry ten times what we paid coming over to get back across the river.

Next connection — a one hour ride on a rusty, sputtering World War II landing craft from Java to the harbor of Lovina on the north shore of Bali.

Most people will tell you that Bali is romantic and most people will talk about the fabulous, lush fauna and the warm, wonderful Balinese people. My version is as close to sheer hell as you can get in that alleged island paradise.

Indonesia is an artificial country, concocted in a speech delivered by an anti-Dutch-Colonialist professor in 1938 to the London School of Economics. "The Archipelago fits together like pieces of a jigsaw puzzle and should be one country" was the argument that he presented. In actuality, many of the islands have nothing in common culturally, historically or religiously. Sumatra is predominately Christian, Bali is mostly Hindu and Muslims or animists inhabit the other islands. During the 1960s the political forces sweeping through this part of the world had spawned the "night of the knives" in Malaysia. One Friday night, after the call to prayers, every Muslim had taken to killing every Chinese in sight across the country in a pre-planned ambush. Indonesia had the same kind of killing spree vetted on their ethnic Chinese population as well. Then the military grabbed 200,000 young Chinese political radicals who were painted with the broad brush of communism and dumped them on the remote rocky atoll known as Bagus.

The Balinese royal family was offered a deal from Jakarta to remain in the Indonesian federation. The Balinese acquiesced at the threat of the barrel of a gun but extracted one promise – that the Indonesia Federation would ethnically cleanse their hated Chinese population.

A human chain of military might swept across the island, giving the Chinese five minutes to pack up whatever they had. The soldiers herded them down to Legian Beach. At the beach there was a large cruise ship a half a mile out at sea. The Chinese were told they were returning to mainland China. Once they got to the other side of the boat, they were then thrown into the sea and drowned. By the end of the day, some of the corpses started to wash ashore, but the beach had been lined with machine guns and those who began to resist were mowed down and pushed out to sea by a bulldozer.

Photographs of this day are displayed on the walls of the National Museum in the town of Solo, Java. It is depicted as a political event, and a counter-revolution. It made me feel creepy, like having a vacation in a World War II death camp.

Daily, all over Bali, hundreds of women brought plates laden with foodstuff and left them at the various idols around the island. I could not stand the idea of such waste. Others thought it archaic or charming.

Bali is a place where animals are chest-deep in grass and where every sort of fruit grew with unimaginable abundance. One could finish a pineapple and stick the leaves in the ground and it would start to grow. Fence posts resembled growing trees when they began to leaf. This great abundance was manifested in these daily offerings. Having been to so many desperately poor places on the planet, I could not enjoy the ritual, thinking it a waste of food. I enjoyed the beach and the waters, for a while, but discovered the hard way that there was a lot of live coral in the ocean. If one wasn't very careful to rinse the ears out after a little session in the surf, the live coral would begin to grow and block the  ear passage. Since no one warned me of this, I had the unhappy experience of having to go to one of the most primitive hospitals in the world and have my ears blown out by a painful jet stream of water.

Rebecca and I left the beach areas and began exploring the highlands of the island. We spent a week in Tampaksiring. The Balinese in the area are known not only for making exotic chess sets with beautifully carved pieces, but as exceptionally skilled, strategic chess players as well. I enjoyed brushing up my moves against such competition. This led to Bali's final insult. The exotic chess set that I commissioned, with a large advance, was never sent. Instead, I got a kind letter every few weeks bemoaning the "delays" and requesting more money. I soon found out from travelers' tales over time, that this was a common occurrence and many who left money had never received their promised chess set.

Chapter Thirty-Six

*"Tibetans say that obstacles in a hard journey, such as
hailstones, wind, and unrelenting rains, are the work of demons,
anxious to test the sincerity of the pilgrims and eliminate the
fainthearted among them"*
"THE SNOW LEOPARD," PETER MATTHIESSEN

I met Capt. David in Nepal. We went trekking to what became the
base camp of the Ganesh Himal, the third highest mountain in
Nepal at more than 25,000 ft. This area had never been open to
trekking. In 1955, a Frenchman named Jes was commissioned by
the King of Nepal to map the area. He was the only Western man
to have ever visited the area before now. David had obtained Jes's
map when he was the captain of a Gurkha Regiment.

David had been kicked out of Sandhurst, the British military
academy equivalent of West Point; and in so doing, earned himself
a commission as a captain in a Gurkha Division in Hong Kong.
The Gurkhas, fierce warriors from the mountains of Nepal, had
worked in the service of the Queen of England since the early
1800s. These mercenaries were originally commissioned by the
crown to rescue a British colonial outpost in India. "Every Gurkha
soldier has been a volunteer, none has ever been a conscript." This
quote is from the Gurkha Museum in Winchester, Hampshire,
U.K. Three thousand Gurkhas stood between the British and a
billion of Chairman Mao's subjects when Captain David arrived in
Asia.

David's assignment in Hong Kong was to don the white uniform and shine. He accompanied a general and his wife when they

attended soirées and meetings with dignitaries or presided over parades and ceremonies. David performed this task well and he enjoyed it. One day, an embittered, unbalanced ethnic Chinese, possibly an agent provocateur, bolted out of a crowd shouting "England out of China," and slashed David across the cheek, leaving a visible scar.

Politically, the British military handled the incident by transferring him to the Gurkha regiment in Nepal – their homeland. The Gurkhas had been promised a pension since the first deal they cut with the British in 1837, when they came down from the Himalayas and rescued the colonial outpost. It was agreed then that they would always be paid only in silver coin. The British kept their end of the deal and Capt. David found himself working with a couple of dozen young guards who carried chests full of silver for delivery to various Gurkha retirement centers in Nepal. Since these retirement centers were often at 14,000 or 15,000 feet, this was not a job done without some care. When David's commitment to the military was fulfilled, he remained in Nepal, enjoying the endless-party lifestyle that had become established by a snobby, European trust-fund contingent. There was no interest in spiritual knowledge, historical research or mountaineering by this social set; they lived for drugs, sex and full moon blow-outs.

Capt. David wanted to go trekking to get away from it all for a while and to get healthy. He painted a convincing verbal picture of mountain scenery and enjoyable rest stops where we could swim or fish for trout.

The Upper Ankola Ganesh Himal was to be officially

opened on April 1 and, as old Asia hands, we were able to offer a small bribe and get a 10-day jump on that date. Captain David, while delivering those coins to the Gurkha retirement centers, had discovered that a trek was enhanced by having one porter carry vodka, another carry chocolate, and a third carry musical instruments. He suggested we try another type of trek that he had always wanted to attempt. We would not go with the high-tech, North Face nylon state-of-the-art gear. We, instead, would travel the old way of the Tibetan nobleman. I agreed and we whistled up his Tibetan mastiff, Nicky, and headed off.

Another reason for our eagerness to be out in the mountains early was we knew there was going to be a full moon eclipse soon and we wanted be as high (altitudinally) as we could before that night. We soon had company. Along the way we were joined by a shaman and his young son at a village up about 8,500 ft. When

the full moon lunar eclipse occurred he performed a fascinating and sacred ceremony. Extracting carved relics, bowls and stones from his bag and placing these objects about himself, he began chanting. He accompanied himself on the sacred drum that he carried on his back at all times. While performing his ceremony, he explained each step to his son, whispering to him the incantations and how to utilize the special objects spread before them.

The villagers we passed were truly excited to see us. At the lower altitudes they were weavers and at the upper altitudes they were subsistence farmers with barley terraces spilling thousands of feet down the mountainsides. This barley, plus meat and yak butter tea, got them through the barren winters. Salty and bitter, yak butter tea actually becomes tasty at higher altitudes.

A Tamang village was the last outpost before the final climb to the proposed base camp site. The people of this village made all of their clothes out of hemp and lived a simple, rugged lifestyle. Tamang means "they came on horses" and yet here they are, subsisting at 16,000 ft. without a horse in sight. They must have eaten those horses, I surmised, after being chased up there by Genghis Khan or some other barbarian conqueror many generations before.

A Tamang offered to take us from this highest village to a nearby hot spring. It was fantastic. We named this spring the "Kathleen de Wilbur Hot Spring" at my suggestion, in honor of the woman who had brought rebirth to the Wilbur Hot Springs out-

side of Calistoga, California. I admired her for undertaking and completing such a major renovation. Naming this uncharted hot spring for her, high in the Ganesh Himal, was an expression of respect. I gave the Tamang man a small Tibetan purse for taking us to the hot spring and he was very pleased because there was nothing colorful in the village.

The next morning we

Our encampment

camped at the proposed base camp site. We were the first trek-kers from outside the region to do so. We pitched our colorful Tibetan-style tents, enjoyed the view and the liquid refreshments Capt. David so wisely brought along. As the porters relaxed, new company arrived.

A Japanese contingent of very orderly climbers must have thought they took a wrong turn when they saw, sprawled on the site of their proposed base camp, an impromptu rhythm band, a ceremonial chillum, a snarling Tibetan mastiff and a slew of slightly tipsy porters. The Japanese could not believe their eyes.

After some awkward and perfunctory polite greetings of mu-tual respect, they had only one question for us. It was translated by their Japanese-speaking Sherpa porters to our English-speak-ing Sherpa porters. That question was "Did you come in by heli-copter?"

"No, we walked here" was our reply, translated back from Sherpa to Sherpa. "Would you care for some chocolate?"

Lower altitude village women weaving and working in the field.

To cross at the highest altitude required a pully-bridge over a gorge thousands of feet deep.

At the last village before base camp, the people survived by making almost everything from hemp. Their simple temple was centuries old.

Chapter Thirty-Seven

"Whatever women do they must do twice as well as men to be thought half as good. Luckily, this is not difficult."
CHARLOTTE WHITTON (1896-1975)

AT THE RANCH, LATE '70S

When you love and marry a girl who already has someone else's child and both her ex and her parents try to take the kid legally you get a job with a major utility. For love, The Sizzler had done just that. "It's the quiet, straight life versus a vindictive, rich, drug-addled former husband plus her parents, who hold dearly to a religious view and who are trying to take the kid!" he said. Three years of emotional turmoil, private investigators, and court appearances had been The Sizzler's challenge. The Sizzler's reward was a two-week vacation from the utility company and he wanted to spend it in Kabul buying carpets.

Najibullah, a leader with one name, now ruled Afghanistan. Najibullah had trained in Moscow and started as the head of the secret police. Being very good at torture, midnight arrests and murder, Najibullah had qualified to move up to puppet Prime Minister.

The Sizz was acutely aware of these facts and added "Najibullah hangs people in the downtown square in Kabul, weekly. That means I can take cash in and throw it around like you did with the Tibetans."

"You might throw something to Ghiaz and Sakhi," I added, as we began quickly working out an arrangement.

When he returned to the United States, Sizz called in with the news – the good, the bad, and the *mupkin* – Farsi for maybe.'The good news was that he had scored great rugs and kept his promise to eye-ball the shipment onto the plane home. The bad news was that Sakhi had been killed by a drunken, staggering soldier just days before the Sizzler arrived in Kabul. The Sizzler said the word was that Sakhi had scolded the soldier for being drunk in public and the soldier had shot him, laughed and moved on. Sakhi's price quotes for hash had been showing up in the trans-global market price guide section of "High Times" magazine. His was the authoritative voice of Afghan hash prices.

It was a couple of days before I could recover from this news and talk to The Sizzler again, when the carpets arrived. Then he gave me the maybe news about seeing Momma and Mona in Kabul. Momma and Mona had kept the false-bottom suitcase makers busy throughout the low-simmering war condition.

The Sizzler said he was incredulous to see Momma and Mona. It was they who told him about Sakhi's murder. Momma also told him that the Amsterdam coffee shops were benefiting from the Afghan political turmoil. Momma and Mona had swept through Kabul and purchased two of the loaded suitcases. But, instead of bringing them into Amsterdam, where the large volume kept the price of hash depressed, Momma told Sizz that she was going to target big American dollars. She and Mona would fly to the U.S.A.

Mona braved American customs and they were successful in making it to California. Everybody was quite ecstatic, including me. Afghan hash had become an unknown entity in the United States. Momma and Mona gave me the suitcases to deal with and they rented a house on the coast. I told them I would be back in a week and I was good to go. When I returned to pay them at their rented house they had a half a dozen men hanging around, ranging in ages from five years younger than Mona to ten years older than Momma. They shooed the men out of the house and we three went out to celebrate.

With great pride and dramatic flare, Momma told us a story. There was an old, very valuable samovar for sale by the only truly upscale diplomatic row antiquities dealer in Kabul. For the diplomats there were some wonderful pieces. At this shop, prices were ten times higher than any dealer in the old Kabul bazaar. The bejeweled centuries-old samovar was for sale for $55,000. It was truly the most prized piece in Afghanistan when we all lived there.

"Everybody wanted that wonderful samovar," said Momma, "especially the smugglers."

"You came up with the $55,000?" I inquired.

"Oh no, because of the war and all the problems – there was even a draft, you know – I was able to get that piece," and she paused with great emphasis, "for around $5,000."

"Only $5,000?!" I was shocked, but not too surprised.

"Lots of beggars and cripples from the war," Mona interjected. "They are desperate for money."

Momma added with a dismissive wave "It's the way of the world. Countries make war and people sell their treasures."

"I understand that," I said, "but still, a museum piece for only $5,000?"

"You must realize one other thing, dah-link," Momma whispered in a hushed, confidential tone. "The man said that for this cheap, cheap price, to make the samovar deal . . . he must have one night with my Mona."

"Oh," I said, somewhat taken aback.

After a brief pause, Mona explained, "Momma said to turn my head and think of something else!"

Chapter Thirty-Eight

*"I'm astounded by people who want to 'know' the universe when
it's hard enough to find your way around Chinatown."*
Woody Allen

The last time we saw the Atman was the following year in Sri
Lanka. The Atman stayed on land in the middle of a National
Wildlife Reserve, outside the important religious town of Kandy.
There were only two other monks allowed to live within the reserve.
Anapanika, a famous German monk and translator of Buddhist
texts, lived in one of the homes. The third resident was a Bikku
who lived in a cave that had, for more than two millennia, been
the home of one monk after another. The British had created the
reserve. The road to the Atman's place was known as Lady Gor-
don's Drive, after the English Viceroy's wife who enjoyed carriage
rides in the area during the British Raj. The reserve bordered one
of the largest botanical gardens ever created by the famed British
botanist, Sir Joseph Hooker. The vast, formal gardens claim to be
home to every known living species of plant. Within ten miles of
our ranch in the California foothills, ironically, there was a tree
named the Hooker Oak, after this same esteemed botanist.

The Atman led us through a series of meditations, practices
and Tantric techniques that were arduous yet enlightening. He
also read and interpreted to us tales of Milarepa, the legendary
poet saint of Buddhism. We also worked on contemplating our
own death and understanding the importance of that inevitability.

He gave me a great deal of insight and a new point of view about my relationship with my son's mother. For me, the difficulty with that relationship was that when I was attentive, I was belittled. When I tried to be sensitive, I was provoked. Conversations were difficult, because topics were changed in mid-sentence.

"It is simple," the Atman explained, "unless she remarries, you are going to have to treat her as if she were your own daughter who has left home and returned with a baby." With that understanding, when I returned to America with this new point of view, it was amazing how quickly the relationship changed for the better.

Chapter Thirty-Nine

"Take a glass of water
Make it against the law
See how good that water tastes
Like you never had it before.
"Bootleg," Credence Clearwater Revival

One summer, most of the Rock and Roll Raj, as the scene now called itself, came to the ranch for a visit. Sweet-and-Sour Sue was living in our Tibetan tent in the garden. Bad Ad, the Shrimp, English Andy and Capt. David showed up. Charmin Carmen, Dean the Dream, Tent Tom and his wife Latchu lived in Northern California, so they were frequent guests.

Visits are an opportunity for growers to exchange information mouth to ear. Bad Ad brought me a few seeds that he found near Gnar, a small village high in the Himalayas. He made the effort to smuggle them in because the plants had noticeably curlicued leaves. Bad Ad did not know if it was an idiosyncrasy or a one-time anomaly. He had grown the variety at his place in Bodnath and the curlicued leaves appeared. I eagerly planted them the following spring and once again, curlicued leaves appeared. However, they were very scrawny and provided little in the way of flowers, even with care and organic soil.

After a major party, the Rock and Roll Raj headed south en-masse to Los Angeles. Somebody had the idea that shooting guns in the desert would be fun and the Kathmandu contingent headed out to blast away on the edge of the LA basin. English Andy was unfamiliar with guns and promptly shot himself in the foot. He was rushed to where the group felt he would receive the best medical attention – a hospital in Beverly Hills. But, the emergency room doctors would not treat Andy after their preliminary examination without a lot of money up front. Also, the docs estimated much more money would be required for what was diagnosed as "extensive rehabilitation" to save the foot. When Andy protested the cost, the LA General Hospital emergency room was suggested. The move probably saved Andy's foot, because the medical team at LA General sees many a gunshot wound. English Andy was cleaned up and on his way in 24 hours for a few hundred bucks.

It was during this week-long party that I revealed to Capt. David many of the ways I had earned money around Asia as, according to Chairman Mao, "a running capitalist dog." Capt. David was minor royalty, a lord of some sort. With it came a natural bearing and panache which I explained to him would go a long way, businesswise, schmoozing customs, bureaucrats and airline agents across Asia.

The opportunities seemed unlimited. I had made a nice profit for a while exporting tropical fish out of Singapore for two reasons. The value of tropical fish in the cold Scandinavian countries is high. First, they were tropical, and second, the death rate in transport was extremely high for such delicate creatures. I figured out that thick plastic and an injection of oxygen into the water carrying the fish, resulted in the death rate being dramatically cut. Before the market took this into account, the profits were outstanding. The Singapore government responded by making it illegal to export many types of fish without a new and expensive license.

Another example of how idiotically politics and economics works was that Tokyo and Beijing are separated by about 800 miles, or two hours by airplane. I was able to buy Japanese watches cheaper in Bangkok than in Japan, because of the incredibly high Japanese domestic sales tax. I then carried two suitcases full of watches in their original cases to Kathmandu, and sold the watches to a local Nawar businessman. I doubled my money. The Nawar would double his money by selling the watches to a Tibetan. The Tibetan would smuggle the watches into occupied Tibet and double his money by selling them to a corrupt Chinese general who would double his money by selling the watches in Beijing.

"How?" you may ask. Because Chairman Mao, in his infinite wisdom, had outlawed private ownership of wrist watches. Mao decreed that public Communist clocks were good enough for anyone who needed to know the time. Punishment for wearing a watch was ten years.

Mao also outlawed pets, other than goldfish. Roses could not be grown. When Mao died, this business was over, but mercifully for us running capitalist dogs, Mrs. Indira Gandhi decided to outlaw gold. Gold in India was, one might say, to a degree worshipped. Gold, like wrist watches, was not illegal in Nepal, Thailand, or any country surrounding India. I went out to the Kathmandu airport to oversee a large shipment of Tibetan carpets being flown out and, as a sidelight, got to observe Dean the Dream shepherd half a dozen trekkers he'd hired in Hong Kong through Nepali customs. They all, including Dean the Dream, had so much gold strapped to their bodies they could hardly walk. I commented that they looked like zombies.

Watches to Beijing, gold to New Delhi or hashish to Amsterdam. Invisible lines and legal loopholes.

The new route to exploit now, I told Capt. David, was Thailand to India. Graciously, the Thais had outlawed the importation of gems from India. One of the keys to invisible line jumping and legal loopholing, I emphasized, was to always look sharp. I, of course, wore a white linen suit.

Chapter Forty

Moulay Ismail, the Sultan of Morocco from 1672-1727,
gifted samples of his bowel movement to the ladies of the court
as a mark of special favor.

Capt. David returned to the Kathmandu area armed with new knowledge and a white suit. He began a successful entrepreneurial life. Unfortunately, the profits could easily be spent in Bangkok, and Bangkok was the downfall of many a good man. Though famous for its fleshpots, bar girls and boys, as well as drugs, the Thai government confines these activities to a very small area that's about two blocks wide and six blocks long. This small geographical area, known as Patpong, is located in the middle of a below-sea level city that rose from a swamp to become a world capital.

Capt. David started flying gems from India. He'd put on the white suit, go to Bangkok and sell them. He'd rage around sin city for a week or two, spending part of the profits, and then fly up to Kathmandu and enjoy a round of the valley's parties before heading back to New Delhi for another easy gem payday.

After wearing the white suit with great success for a year, the debauchery that accompanied that success caught up with him in India. Capt. David was arrested trying to leave New Delhi with a suitcase full of gems and taken to prison. The white suit was stained with brandy, mud, soy sauce, ketchup, cigarette burns and probably cum, which likely tipped off a customs inspector.

Unfortunately, Capt. David's arrest photo looked like a movie-star version of an English jewel thief. Each day his story grew in the India media. The exaggerated version sold lots of newspapers. When Indian television picked up the fact that David had a minor English royal title, the local daily news programs broadcast breaking-news angles of yet another rare jewel that had been stolen from some Maharaja or other in the 1950s and now discovered amongst the decadent playboy's loot.

Capt. David's two best friends were Bad Ad and English Andy. They brought in Big Red Ted and Dutch Bob to try and figure out a way to get him out of Tihar prison. His family employed a high-powered Indian lawyer. The problem was you could not bribe the warden of Tihar prison. Indira Gandhi's India had a very watchful eye on the finances of their high officials.

Money had been spent to purchase David better conditions in the jail. He was taken out of his cell for a few hours in the afternoon and chained by the ankle to a huge spreading, sprawling banyan tree growing in one of the prison's yards. The murderer Charles Sobhraj was in the same prison. Sobhraj was allowed to collect money for interviews and potential documentaries and books on his life. He spent some of it building a platform eight feet high in the branches of the same banyan tree that David was shackled to. Sobhraj was shackled as well, but being up in the tree relieved him of the mental duty of constant concern for rat attack. Sobhraj hated David's competing notoriety. He began to defecate on his platform and throw the result down through the branches, where inevitably a bit would hit its mark.

Big Red Ted asked me to come in and make a contribution. Bill Wassman had already been banned for life from India for his earlier, small-time hash arrest. I flew into New Delhi from California and met with the lawyer. With great flourish, the attorney explained that he had tried bargaining with some high-level politician to arrange a pardon or a deportation, but David had made some very derogatory, racist comments to his original arresting officers and they really wanted to pound some English, former-colonialist flesh. "Five years," he concluded.

This was the first time I'd been in India when it wasn't by choice. That is a bad, bad feeling. I was itchy, edgy and could not sleep. I was afraid I might get caught up in some international drug agent intrigue and find myself in jail. It takes a two-week stay in the labyrinth that is Tihar prison before your home country Embassy representative can see you.

At 4:00 A.M., lying on a sticky, sweaty, musty Indian sheet in a no-star hotel, the Mother of Invention whispered, "You must ask!" I went back to see the lawyer. Once again the barrister professed his extraordinary legal skills. His remarkable legal ability could keep David's jail time to "only five years!" he reiterated. With the full knowledge that I might be eating chapatti and drinking rancid water soon, I popped the question, "what would the warden take if it isn't money?"

"Gasoline," he said. "It is rationed in India but monitored less carefully than money; the warden of Tihar prison loves to chauffer his two daughters around town on Sunday afternoons . . . I make a little joke, of course."

I managed a little laugh for his benefit and left.

Two weeks later, under a full moon, at the India/Nepal border, English Andy, Bad Ad, and Big Red Ted watched four elephants, with four border-knowledgeable mahouts astride, cross into India. One elephant also carried one powerful Nepalese politician. Each elephant carried 50 Jerry-cans of gasoline.

Forty-eight hours later, at the same border crossing, Red Ted, being the biggest, had the money for the final payoff Ace-bandaged around his calves. Andy had a bottle of Courvoisier cognac in hand; and Bad Ad held a bottle of Johnny Walker Red, the *special* favorite of the powerful Nepalese official who had crossed into India with the gasoline two nights before.

Out of the night came the four elephants, driven by the four border-knowledgeable mahouts. The elephants carried the same powerful, Nepalese, Johnny-Walker-loving politician, plus his cousin/brother, who happened to be a powerful, local, Courvoisier cognac-loving Indian official . . . and one bedraggled Brit wearing Sobhraj-shit-speckled clothes.

Chapter Forty-One

*"I knew that I was an unwanted baby when I saw that my bath
toys were a toaster and a radio."*

JOAN RIVERS

Rebecca and I were wandering through Durbar Square, in
downtown Kathmandu, where there was always a wealth
of human activity. On this day, there was more life than usual
because the town was gearing up for Shiva Ratri. For this holiday,
thirty to forty thousand *sadhus* complete a pilgrimage to Kathmandu to celebrate Shiva's birthday. The festival takes place in a
sacred area along the Bagmati River at the Pashupatinath Temple.
With Shiva Ratri only a week away, there were plenty of colorful,
bizarre holy men gathered when Ira and Petra drove up.

Ira and Petra cut quite a social swath in the ex-pat community. Ira was a photographer who specialized in the weird. He would
take snaps of beggars who had purposefully deformed themselves
or *sadhus* who had pierced their scrotum or penis. One *sadhu* had
attached a small wagon to his penis and walked backwards to attend. As a result, his member looked like a spaghetti noodle and
ended below his knees.

Petra dressed 1940s New York City; a pillbox hat, veil and
padded-shoulder camel hair overcoat with velvet trim. Ira dressed
real sporty as well. The couple always arrived in a 1950 cream-
colored Cadillac that they had acquired from some fallen-on-hard-
times Nepali and restored to pristine running condition. Most of

the exiles in the Valley at that time dressed for comfort, depending on how hot or cold the temperature was.

Ira moved through the crowd snapping shots of various oddities with Petra in tow. Rebecca and I watched them approach a beggar who had a small girl with him. The small girl had a kitchen fork piercing her tongue. Ira snapped a photo of her. As we arrived within earshot and stopped short, awestruck, Petra was discovering the little girl's mother had died in childbirth in a village in India – two thousand miles from where she now stood. When she was six years old, her father had a vision that if he made the pilgrimage to Pashupatinath for the Lord Shiva's birthday celebration, good fortune would prevail for himself and his daughter. Unfortunately, the price his daughter had to pay to attend this event was the improvised trident (a Hindu religious symbol of Shiva) that pierced her tongue. This physical symbol allows begging and usually garners more money. The little girl had walked two thousand miles with the trident in her tongue, while her father begged their way to Kathmandu. It had taken a year, yet they managed to arrive ten days early.

The girl's father finished the story in broken English with much hand emphasis, while his daughter continued to work the crowd for coins. Petra and Ira adopted the child on the spot. With little fanfare, they left in the old Caddie and headed to the doctor to have the fork removed. The next time we saw this lovely girl, she was riding a mountain bike and had Nepali-girl golden bands from elbow to wrist.

Chapter Forty-Two

"Oh, East is east and West is west,
And never the twain shall meet
Till earth and sky stand presently at God's great judgment seat."
RUDYARD KIPLING

Shiva Ratri was nothing less than an incredible experience. The exile crowd erected a couple of roomy Tibetan tents on a flat spot above the humanity at the temple below. Giant stone stairs spilled down to the river and when the event officially kicked off, thousands of already frantic Kathmandu citizens rushed down for a frantic few seconds of splashing some special water manna on themselves; then they were off through the continuous parade to the various sacred sites of the temple area. To be a *sadhu,* one only had to renounce one's worldly possessions. A sadhu's sole possessions are his robe, a begging bowl, a pouch of the sacramental hashish or ganja and a stick to beat off village dogs and to support himself during his pilgrimages. Besides these holy men, Jains, Zoroasters and representatives of smaller religious sects from all over India were there. They dressed in a myriad of styles that represented the official clothing of their particular role or station in the various religions. Rather than have his iron will flaunted, the King of Nepal officially declared the use of *charas* legal for the three-day celebration. The Nepali police took advantage of the King's decree by joining in the festivities and mixing with the smokers, *sadhus* and citizens.

Shiva Ratri provided many weird and memorable moments.

One such was Ram Ness, who was in charge of burning corpses. This was an important position, but nonetheless, filled by the lowest caste in the Hindu system that still strongly prevails in Nepal as well as India. Besides burning corpses, Shiva Ratri was the only other big thing that Ram Ness had going on in his, at best, dreary life. Thousands upon thousands of believers, who never visited Ram Ness' part of the vast temple complex, streamed past his cave-like dwelling located in front of the burning ghats. His *ga-rungs* or tough guys, were in charge of moving the corpses about for thorough, efficient cremation. They were members of his caste and were hardened by centuries of civilization's rejection of them and their forebears. Ram Ness rewarded the passing religious revelers, who threw money at him, either by floating naked in a big tub, standing up to fart in their direction or hopping out of the tub and pointedly throwing their paper money back at them and into the cooking fire. The *garungs* would scowl at the passing throng as Ram Ness berated, spit and scoffed at them.

Bad Ad was a Cajun who spoke with a soft, Southern patois. He had shown me many an odd ritual festival or historical site during our friendship. He was fluent in Tibetan and Nepali and could translate Ram Ness' coarse screed. "He's calling them mother rapers and donkey sodomizers." At one point, Bad Ad told me, "Now he's telling some people that they are going to die from rectal cancer."

We wandered over to a group of *Charas Baba's* and Bad Ad snapped some pictures of me. This may have been when he got, shall we say, not the best of ideas.

"The favored *garung* gets to taste a bit of his work. I wanna photo-document it. One shot plucking a bit of the corpse; a second shot in his hand and a third going into his mouth."

"A little taste of his work?" I gagged.

"Photo-journalism, my man . . . of different cultural phenomena," he said in the soft accent. "Hell, I'll be lucky to get one photo of Ram Ness," Bad Ad declared. "Ram Ness *forbids* photos."

I noticed that the *gurangs* did rush out to deter the tourists the second they got a glimpse of a camera.

Bad Ad had been living in the

Kathmandu Valley long enough to know both the Nepali and Tibetan languages. He was well-steeped in both cultures and ways since he lived on an extremely limited budget himself. So when he said "Ram Ness forbids it," and that he was going to try and get a photo anyway, I knew he was floating a trial balloon at me to see at what level I would get involved. "I need you to be a diversion," he said with a smile.

"I'll try and be a help, but those *garungs* look like they're over amped on the no-photo-deal," I replied.

Bad Ad said "I'll just go down to the river's edge and use my telephoto lens, grab a couple of snaps and move on. This is what I need you to do: A) have a few rupees in your hand, B) stand about ten yards back from the Ram Ness cave, and C) if you see the *garungs* actually charge me . . . D) throw a few rupees down on the ground for distraction to give me a head start to escape."

I did as requested. I stood about ten yards away and when the *garungs* charged, I scattered the rupees. One of them stopped to pick up the money, but the other four or five charged straight on to Bad Ad. One got behind him and put shaved bamboo down his neck. Bad Ad could only do one thing – pull his hooded sweatshirt off! Shaved bamboo is the world's most intense itching powder. When that hooded sweatshirt went above his head, the sticks and the fists pummeled him backwards. One *garung* grabbed his shoulder bag and another his camera, while two others threw Bad Ad into the river. It was over in seconds.

Bad Ad had two new requests for me: getting as much water as possible on the itchy spot and then getting out of there and somewhere dry.

Chapter Forty-Three

"Our ignorance of history makes us libel our own times.
People have always been like this."
GUSTAVE FLAUBERT (1821-1880)

I was invited to show slides of the Ganesh Himal trek at the American Embassy in Kathmandu in celebration of the 1776 American Bicentennial. The stars of the event were the American Mountaineering Team that climbed Mt. Everest and planted the stars and stripes for the anniversary. The slide show was the opening act for the climbers 35mm film entitled "Assault on Everest." The title fit perfectly into the long tradition of putting a military spin on everything American.

The *common man* spin was applied to the Embassy affair. They served chili dogs, French fries and, the big surprise, Coors beer! Allegedly, the beer came to Nepal on a refrigerated plane directly from Colorado. It was silly, but benign compared to what previous American Presidents had dealt Asia.

Back in 1974, then-President Ford and Henry Kissinger, the two most powerful representatives of the USA, had showed up in Jakarta, Indonesia, while we were there. They spent less than 24 hours in Jakarta before heading on to Vladivostok for a meeting with Leonid Brezhnev, then the ruler of the USSR. The next day, the Indonesian army attacked the island of Timor and spawned a new war. Who knows if they ordered it or just gave it the okay?

We went to Burma during this time of manufactured political

turmoil. Burma had its share of woe as well. Travelers were allowed only one week in that country and only one visit per year.
Burma had stopped foreigners from visiting in 1947, after it
gained independence from Britain after WWII. Like Cubans, Bur-
mans were famous for still driving pre-1950 American cars.

In Burma, our interest was in getting up to Pagan. Pagan had
16 square miles of golden temples, each more grand than the next.
Some of the temples had gone back to nature, occupied by wildlife, vegetation and dangerous snakes. Others were maintained
in pristine condition. It looked as though for 350 years there had
been a frenzy of Buddhist temple building. It was often said that
Pagan was actually one of the Wonders of the World and the fact
that no British adventurer had ever discovered it was the only
reason there were not Eight Wonders. It was energizing. I rented
horses and it was a good way to cover a lot of history and marvel
at the scenery since there was only a few hundred yards between
each edifice. One temple had four, 65 ft, solid gold Buddha statues
facing in the cardinal directions.

Marco Polo had been the original Westerner to venture
through. Here is what he said, from the "Travels of Marco Polo:"
"The towers are built of fine stone and then one of them has been
covered with gold, a good finger in thickness, so that the tower
looks as if it were all of solid gold. And the other towers covered
with silver in like manner, so it seems to be all of solid silver. They
formed one of the finest sites in the world, so exquisitely furnished
are they, so splendid and costly. And when they are lighted up by
the sun, they shine most brilliantly and are visible from a vast
distance."

We stayed at Tony's Rest House. Tony helped us find the
horses and was certainly glad to see us up there in that remote,
politically volatile land, so cut off from the rest of the planet.
Tony's Rest House was run by the son of Tony, named Tony Jr.
As we ate our dinner, consisting of noodles and small fried fish
from the Irawaddy River, Tony Jr. hollowed out a Burmese cigar

and stuffed it full of what I can only call commercial swamp weed. When we finished eating, he lit it up and offered it to us with a flourish, saying "In Pagan, this is what we call dessert!"

Another highlight of the trip was our voyage up the Irawaddy River with a native boatman who knew all the tiny currents in the broad, slow river. He moved us along, criss-crossing with pole and paddle from the city of Pagan to the Temple of One Thousand Stairs. When the Buddha, spreading the dharma, had come to the Pagan area, he had never really been on the lowland plain where all the Buddhist temples are built, but rather, stood on a cliff high above the river ten miles south of the city. This is where the great temple was built in Buddha's name. It was designed, auspiciously, with the correct number of stairs to make the pilgrim pay a small price to remember the arduous effort of the Buddha to bring the Dharma to such a remote place.

There was also a twenty-unit government hotel that shuttled in tourists on a very crowded and harried schedule, taking them on a three-day run out of Rangoon up to Pagan, around Mandalay and back. That was about the only money making it to Northern Burma – except for the dirty little war.

In Burma, the war was waged against the ethnic Karens, a people who lived in the teakwood forests of the North. The name "Burma" came from the ethnic group the "Burman" that controlled the port of a delta area at the Bay of Bengal. The British named the country after those Burman, since they were the only ones they did business with. The Burman liked to take the teak, denuding the landscape of the Karen people. If the Karen got in the way, they were chopped down just like trees.

Most British descriptions of the countryside were "it's mud or dust." They preferred the wide streets and civility of Rangoon. A calming influence did prevail in the city, likely due to the elaborate and ornate Shre Daargron temple complex. The Shre Daargron stupa has magnificent, pure gold spires that can be seen from commercial jet airliners at 40,000 feet.

Rebecca and I spent only one day of the allowed seven in Rangoon on our first trip, but I scoped out a lot of prime, museum-quality historical finds. When I returned to Burma, exactly one year after my new visa would allow, I purchased a first edition of Longfellow's "The Wreck of the Hesperus," printed in 1839 and complete with illustrations.

Rangoon Waterfront

Monks at a horse cart taxi stand

Though Burma is one of the most impoverished nations, it is home to the most ornate Temples

Chapter Forty-Four

"Mind Moves the Mass"
MOTTO, UNIVERSITY OF OREGON

Statthakis, an FM radio interviewer who went by that one name alone, was a well-known socialist gadfly and political prankster in Eugene, Oregon. He was popular enough in Eugene to have finished third when he ran for mayor of the town. He invited me to read my poetry at Ken Kesey's poetry Hoo Ha at Mac Court on the University of Oregon campus. Alan Ginsberg and Gregory Corso were the featured poets and I was thrilled to be able to mingle with them, as well as Kesey. Accompanying Ginsberg was his long-time partner, Peter Orlovsky, playing the harmonium. Corso, agitated

Max Gail and Singer Laura Allen backstage

and edgy, quickly read two poems, and without another word, left the stage and the state. Any hopes of reminiscing or peeling the intellectual onion with Kesey were dashed due to his psychedelicized state.

Later that evening, I met an aspiring actor, Max Gail. Max had just completed a pilot episode playing a wacky detective for a sitcom "Barney Miller." Max was a warm man, thoroughly moved to help people and save the planet. Max also expressed concern that if successful, he was going to be branded a TV celebrity and denied his true desire to perform in musical comedy. We were in a hot tub in the expansive back yard of a wealthy patron of the arts who was throwing the Hoo-Ha after-party. There was a piano in the living room and to emphasize his career desire, Max left the hot tub, grabbed a towel and went to the piano and adeptly belted out a few show tune standards. We became friends and later did some socializing back in the Bay area.

The "Barney Miller" sitcom became an immediate success and Max bought a modest bungalow in Point Dume, a small town north of Malibu. Max invited me down to check it out. Bob Dylan's house was under construction when we were in Yalapa; now it was finished and only two blocks away. It was prominent in the little hamlet for its copper cupola. Jim Franklin's armadillo mural decorated the bottom of the swimming pool. Max also became friends with Martin Sheen. Sheen had a basketball hoop on the driveway and he hosted neighborhood pickup games. His two sons, Charlie and Emilio, were avid young players and because I was taller and Emilio younger, we would find ourselves in spirited competition with Martin and his older son, Charlie.

Max Gail was a serious man. His foremost cause was improving the plight of Native Americans. His Point Dume home soon became a refuge for young Native Americans who were disoriented in the transition from reservation life to the modern urban jungle. Max had a sweat lodge in his yard to help purify their bodies and spirit, as well as his own.

Another life-or-death issue for Max that I shared was the No Nukes movement. I had seen photographs of barrels of nuclear waste that, in the 1950s, had been foolishly dumped off the Farallon Islands, just twenty-seven miles from San Francisco. Graham

Nash had penned the lyrics to "Barrel of Pain," a song that dealt specifically with this human time-bomb:

> "I can see the sea begin to glow
> I can feel it leaking down below!
> I can barely stand it
> What you're doing to me
> And in the morning will you still feel the same?
> How you going to keep yourself
> From going insane
> With glowing children and a barrel of pain."

Martin Sheen was in the forefront of the No Nukes movement and he invited Max and and me to physically assist at the "No Nukes" concert at Madison Square Garden. Spearheaded by Jon Hall, the concert ran for five days and raised nationwide awareness of the pitfalls and the extremely long-term, inherent dangers, of improperly used nuclear energy.

I experienced one gathering in Max's sweat lodge. It was conducted by Floyd "Red Crow" Westerman. During the ritual, I was struck by the similarity of it to one of my sessions with the Atman in Asia. Westerman tossed bits of sage, tobacco and other substances on the hot rock fire. The resulting smoke and the aromatic aura of this concoction seemed to create introspective insights and self-evaluations that bubbled through the brain in a similar, transcendent manner.

Chapter Forty-Five

"A bit of fragrance always clings to the hand that gives roses."
Chinese Proverb

Just when my son was starting first grade, his mother and I worked out the first steps of custody and legalities. Her attorney asked for a private moment with my lawyer and me.

"My client says to remind you that your attorney is representing the 'Bandit of Kabul.' She says that will hasten the process in this matter."

When you are growing marijuana in your backyard, you don't have a lot of leverage. As I accepted the deal, I thought back to The Sizzler living a quiet, caring life for his adopted child. I chose to follow The Sizzler's example from that moment on.

I got the privilege of taking my boy anywhere in three Bay Area counties. The San Francisco 49ers, Oakland A's, Giants, Warriors, beaches, hiking trails, museums, and sailboats, all offered choices for father/son exploration.

William VIII's widow, Aggie, was raising William IX in a Northern California beach town. My son and his mother moved there as well. There was a great little school in the district with only a dozen kids in each classroom and lots of green grass and a view of a wild life lagoon. It seemed like a perfect school. Coincidently, Jerry Garcia and Mountain Girl were living in the same town with their two daughters, who were approximately the same age as both boys. He would mention his reccurring disappointment with Rabid Ron, from the Hooteroll session days. Rabid Ron had absconded with $240,000 of the Grateful Dead's record company royalties and disappeared to Europe.

I would run into Gracia at the little beach town's only general store, deli and booze shop. I told him from my own, now considerable, Asia knowledge and perspective . . . how pulling off the Dead concert at the Egyptian pyramids would historically become a greater and greater achievement. People would understand the incredible logistics, bizarre foreign bureaucracies, and jet lag twilight zone it must have become and yet they still made music.

It made him very happy. On another occasion I showed him a photo of the "Keep on Truckin'" patch on my jeans at the bottom of the Ajanta Pass on the Old Silk Road.

"Let the freak flag fly," with a warm smile, was Garcia's exit line.

Sadly for Jerry, his family was forced to move. Month after month an incessant trail of Deadheads continually camped out in the woods, on the beach and even right in front of Jerry's garage. Mountain Girl could not tolerate this kind of madness. It was particularly poignant for me. Whatever the interaction between the adults there was one thing I could be very sure of: those four chil-

Keep On Truckin' Patch on Silk Route Ride

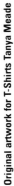
Original artwork for T-Shirts Tanya Meade

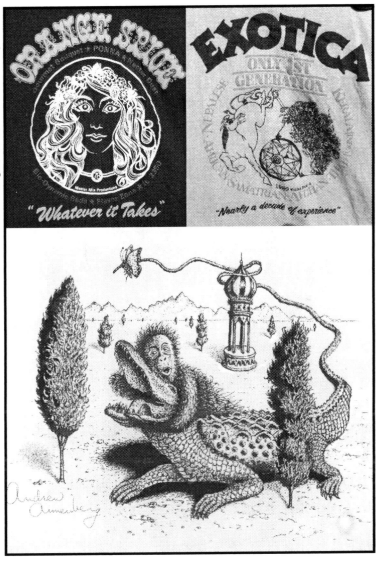

dren felt lots of love and affection for each other. Having Jerry and Mountain Girl move away resulted in losing the dynamic of a "big extended family" relationship, something I felt strongly should be present in child rearing.

Our friends from Kabul, German Ted, Tory, and their child Guava, had not been so lucky while in the States. In our hearts,

Tory, a pioneering woman, will always be remembered as she was galloping to safety from the Afghan village mob attack. She was fearless and skilled enough to be out there in harm's way – a feminist's dream. The traveling community also remembered Tory for her fine, artistic embellishments on the hashish disks. Unfortunately, a patron of her art kept one of the discs for many years and was eventually arrested for growing an indoor pot garden. He offered to give up an "international operation" in return for leniency and named Tory.

German Ted, from whom Tory had split in Afghanistan, tried to make amends with her in her time of crisis. He rushed to her aid via Canada. Officials were waiting for him. Unbeknownst to Ted, he was on an Interpol watch list because of the informing rat's treachery. A month in jail and deportation to Germany for Ted was the result. For Tory, a first-rate mother and a compassionate, artistic soul, a year's hard time.

Chapter Forty-Six

"Oh, I am just a vagabond, a drifter on the run
And eloquent profanity, it rolls right off my tongue
Yes, I have dined in palaces, drunk wine with kings and queens
But darlin' oh darlin' you're the best thing I ever seen.
Won't you roll 'em easy, so slow and easy?
Take my independence with no apprehension, no tension
Because you are a walkin', talkin' paradise, sweet paradise."
"ROLL 'EM EASY," LITTLE FEAT

In 1980, when Jimmy Carter bid adieu to the political scene and Ronnie Reagan ascended, America looked like it would get a chance to have a government that wasn't going to use war as its major instrument of policy.

Our ranch had acres of French biodynamic gardens, forty fruit and nut trees, and all summer long there were thirty or forty swimmers splashing in the creek. Kids and dogs were a daily delight. The rock and roll shows were steady and successful, reggae was firmly entrenched in the scene and people such as the creative, innovative, highly skilled Tom Ness, Bill Bunn and Laurie Bell had left their mark. They were true believers in green, organic gardening.

The Appaloosa breed of horse, with its gentle disposition and affectionate nature, evolved into the horse of choice for the ranch. Known for its sure-footed ability, it proved to be perfect for the shale and slightly treacherous terrain of the foothills. Andrew Annenberg captured it all perfectly with his illustrations for our t-shirt. The gardens and the t-shirts had become an institution. The Tibetan carpets sold steadily. Rebecca organized summer

camps for all the nieces and nephews and the neighboring children, where they learned old-fashioned crafts, enjoyed swimming
in the creek and horseback riding. Kachook loved children, cats
and colts. As promised for saving us that horrible, desperate night
in Afghanistan, Kachook was spared a life as a chained, mindless
beast or fighting dog. His dog's life's highlight was likely when on
a twilight hike in the canyon we came upon a mountain lion. Without hesitation, Kachook charged and treed the big cat. He did not
fare so well on a chance encounter with a bear, however, as the

big beast rolled Kachook with one swat of its mighty paw and then raked the dog's underbelly with sharp claws. Kachook was lucky to survive and fully recover.

Here in America, family problems now seemed trivial compared to what the teeming masses in Asia lived through. At any time in Asia you were close to the Endless War. You would hear it from the survivors. "Out of nowhere bombs, napalm or chemicals," they'd say, pointing at the sky.

In 1978, the Church Commission offered a peek at the mayhem unleashed, unbridled on Asia. The Plain of Jars, a plateau in Laos, received more bombs from 1950–1959 than the U.S. dropped in all of World War II.

"Disparate boat people" was what the international media dubbed the many suffering souls who were fleeing to their deaths like lemmings in small boats. They were escaping from a napalm-burned, Agent Orange-carcinogized infrastructure; their home now a destroyed-planet zone.

It can roll through your mind for days when, while hunkered down in a noodle shop with the owner, waiting out a torrential rain squall, and the conversation goes . . . "I am boy in Cambodia and BOOM, leg of cow . . . my family cow . . . BOOM . . . into house and kill mother. Cow leg kills her! Why America drop bomb on Cambodia?"

Five-hundred-and-forty-thousand tons of bombs is the official figure. 540,000 tons of hot, murderous steel.

We who lived Asia knew what a hand-to-mouth and month-to-month existence the people had in the best of times. A family cow, blown up from 36,000 feet above, if not killing the noodle shop man's mother, would have likely caused her and his little sister and old grandmother to starve to death because of the loss of their main form of sustenance. Obesity, on the other hand, was a major problem for American kids.

The kid and I caught a break, however . . . mom had taken refuge in Buddhism. It still left a problem and it was not obesity,

nor was it trivial. My boy's mother had decided, in her true, wom-
en's lib fashion, that competition in young boys only led to war.
My young son was, therefore, never going to play Little League,
basketball or any such thing. But, hey, he was living in a beach
town in California and if you don't learn how to play in the pickup
basketball leagues, and eventually surf – you're probably going to
be eating anti-depressants and boozing it up like the bored, un-
fulfilled teenagers of the town. Also, the legal hammer came down
heavy – I could only take my son into the three adjoining counties
during my allowed visitation. My ranch was inconveniently out of
range of the legal ruling.

In a touch of irony, I was recruited as the referee for the first
annual Earth Ball game where, in a field near the Golden Gate
Bridge, a hundred kids pushed a gigantic ball around the Marin
Headlands – good exercise but with no real athletic purpose. On
my referee's tee shirt were the rules of the game – Have Fun, Play
Fair and Don't Get Hurt.

When I was not with my son I was busy researching the bio-
active qualities of marijuana. This study kept me constantly involved in improving and understanding my plants. Cannabis has
been used in Chinese medicine for centuries to induce appetite
and combat eye pressure related to glaucoma. I was determined
to learn more about the ubiquitous weed.

Montreal Michael came to the ranch for a visit and brought a
box full of research and clinical studies on cannabis. Tantalizing
evidence was coming forward that showed benefits for the nervous
system and disorders such as ALS, or Lou Gehrig's disease as
it is commonly known. This knowledge was particularly dear to
me since my uncle Ken's horrible demise from a similar disorder,
Huntington's chorea, which could be passed on genetically.

Michael also brought photos of his wife and the ninety-three
foot yacht they were living on in Singapore harbor. In his own ex-
acting and unique style he had personally chosen the teak trees
from the Malaysian jungle and employed local Malay ship build-

ers to create the magnificent vessel from Vancouver blueprints. He and his wife, Lacie, lived on board the yacht and made a living moving cargo through various Asian ports. Unfortunately the seeds he bought to be planted for his research were opium seeds. When he hinted that occasionally his cargo was opium and there was room for an associate, I offered my well-known-to-him moral objection to any substance that enslaves the human spirit. He took offense, repackaged the research and rather abruptly left the ranch.

By the end of that summer, Rebecca's and my own hopes for having a child came to a sad and unfulfilling end. After a good deal of medical procedure and attempts for pregnancy at great cost, it became a no go. Rebecca had issues from a burst appendix in her early teens and it had come back to haunt us. Though she could not have a child of her own, her personal pain from that sad realization was tempered by her fulfilling and loving contribution to my son's well being.

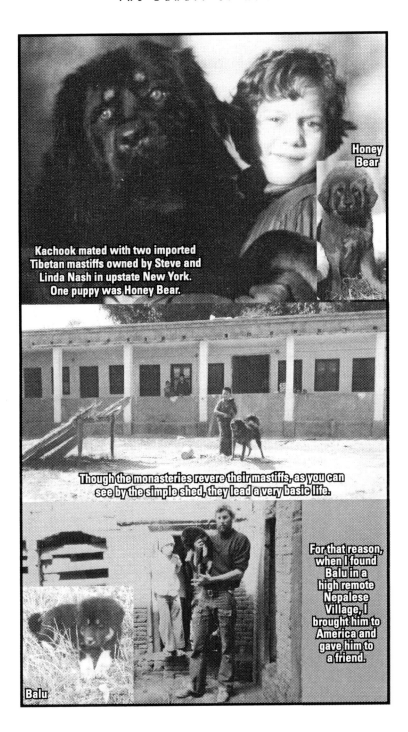

Honey Bear

Kachook mated with two imported Tibetan mastiffs owned by Steve and Linda Nash in upstate New York. One puppy was Honey Bear.

Though the monasteries revere their mastiffs, as you can see by the simple shed, they lead a very basic life.

For that reason, when I found Balu in a high remote Nepalese Village, I brought him to America and gave him to a friend.

Balu

Chapter Forty-Seven

"Let your mind be as a floating cloud. Let your stillness be as the
wooded glen. And sit up straight.
You'll never meet the Buddha with such bad posture."
THE LOTUS & THE MISHPOKKEH – THE PRINCIPLES OF JEWISH BUDDHISM

In 1979, Tenzin Gyatso, the 14th Dalai Lama of Tibet, made his first visit to America. My friend Big Red Ted had occasionally served as His Holiness' translator/bodyguard in Europe and Asia. Ted spoke the "high Lhasa" dialect of the language of Tibet and it was through his contacts that we were able to meet with His Holiness on his first visit to the U.S. The meeting took place at a Methodist church located in rural, bucolic New Jersey. It was a beautiful, sunny day with a perfect little breeze on the textured green garden-like grounds. Most of the Americans who were present had already taken refuge in the Buddhist philosophy. Bill Wassman and I hadn't. We didn't have the courage.

A commercial 747 jet airliner delivered His Holiness to the heart of the planet's greatest Western power. President Jimmy Carter recently achieved an incremental gain to stop the USA's endless war on third world countries. It did appear that nuclear non-proliferation made some headway during Carter's term.

Before the ceremony began the gathering was much like any holiday picnic. Energetic kids played on the grounds and there was abundant Tibetan style food such as *tsampa*, butter tea and *momos*. Local gossip punctuated the political discussions. We were amazed to see a dozen or so of the most successful of our Tibetan comrades from the carpet trade. They were thrilled to make their first visit to the West and to physically support the opportunity it presented to internationalize the plight of their homeland. Seeing the Dalai Lama in America, their hope soared with great, shared joy. The refugees living in the States and the knowledgeable Westerners in attendance also shared a gestalt coming out of the now-familiar, ancient Buddhist prophecy: "When the Iron Bird flies and the Horse runs on wheels, the Tibetans will be scattered like ants across the face of the earth."

His Holiness addressed the audience and conducted a magnificent, ancient religious ceremony. There was an extraordinary oneness permeating from his message as it was amplified from a stage in New Jersey. It seemed every Tibetan refugee who had been relocated to the United States was there and was beaming as if reborn. Most had endured incredible hardships and had refugee status early in life, so for them this was a momentous day.

Ted had promised Bill and me that we would have an opportunity to meet the Dalai Lama. Ted offered Bill this "tease" in order to ensure that Bill did the driving and that I pitched in on a rental car to take us to the ceremony. The Dalai Lama was not yet a media super-star, but Bill and I would probably have traveled by Greyhound bus to the event.

Ted was true to his word. When the opportune moment arose, he slipped us in to meet Tenzin Gyatso, the 14th Dalai Lama of Tibet.

Ted introduced us as long-time friends of Tibet and great trekking aficionados. He also explained that I had researched and written a scholarly work on the Tibetan mastiff. It was a most uplifting and cordial exchange. His Holiness gave us a specific mantra and told Ted to translate it into written English. Ted fidgeted for paper and ultimately settled on a corner of the day's program, writing, *Om Ah Rapatsanadhi.* The part of this Buddhist prayer that Ted translated on the spot was, "Here I totally, completely, vanquish desire and hatred." The prayer came from the Manju

Bodhisattva. Ted said he'd tell us the whole thing later and shooed us out. The white scarves known as *katas* that are used for greetings and departures, were draped around our necks by the Dalai Lama's secretary, Rinchin Darlo.

The grounds were nearly empty when Ted came out to meet us and to make the drive back to New York City. The car was full of the most exciting and excited conversations. Ted, demanding a solemn moment, expanded on the Dalai Lama's meditation that he had transcribed for us. Explaining that we had now been charged with a new role in life, Red Ted said, "The Dalai Lama's reference to the Bodhisattva Manjurshri when he spoke to you two bozos is important! It means: Use the flaming sword of knowledge to strike down the fearsome foe . . . but leave out the enmity of the mind."

Bill, always the sly quipster, asked, "Is that fearsome foe a drunken hillbilly coming at you with a tire iron in one hand and a broken beer bottle in the other?"

"No," said Ted patiently, "that foe is the ignorance of the agitated mind."

Chapter Forty-Eight

"He went to Europe as a boy, where in Geneva his father arranged for a prostitute. He was so terrified by the experience that he didn't marry until he was 67 years old."

JOHN LEONARD IN A NEW YORK TIMES BIOGRAPHICAL REVIEW OF THE SOUTH AMERICAN WRITER AND CRITIC, JORGE BORGES

There was always something new in the ever-evolving parental custody situation. Here was a surprise twist: My son and his mother were moving onto the premises of a mansion in the Santa Barbara hills. It was owned by an ardent women's liberationist who had major money. There were three or four small houses that were occupied by single women with sons. These boys were going to be given the best vegetarian foods and pre-school education and prevented from having any part of macho, knuckle-dragging eager soldiers and killers. The trust-fund money financed a long list of beliefs that included the conditioning out of the American male child such things as competition, hunting, and football. These women were going to save as many as they could. I went down and checked it out and saw that it was some of the nicest bunch of first-class nonsense that any boy could enjoy for a year or two. I was right, and in less than a couple of years they had left those high rolling Santa Barbara hills and returned to the "valley of the million-dollar brown shingle bungalow."

Mom had access to a legal aid attorney who specialized in single parent custody cases and it only cost her $20.00 a session. I paid the standard rate of $100 an hour in the ongoing custody negotiations. Ouch!

I did begin, at this time, a long-term strategy to make sure Little League baseball would be in my son's future. I explained here and there, whenever I could, that baseball was a game that taught humility. A game, that if you were very successful, you succeeded three or four times out of ten. Also, I pointed out the choreographed ballet that was necessary for youngsters to safely practice this sport. From the very beginning, the young participants were taught that they could not wildly either throw the ball or swing the bat, and that everything from the way the ball was thrown after an out was made, or where the next batter stood to take their practice swings, was designated and designed.

I knew that if I could just get my son into that first uniform, it would melt his mother's heart like millions before. Also, as it should be, the child should finally decide and in this case no sweeter words ever came to my ears than "I'm gonna play in the Little League!"

Chapter Forty-Nine

"GOD! . . . The country that produced George Washington
has got this collection of crumb-bums!"
THE BRILLIANT HISTORIAN, BARBARA TUCHMAN, ON THE 1980 ELECTION

In 1981, I was a volunteer at Peace Sunday. Peace Sunday was held at the Rose Bowl and had 106,000 attendees. Peace Sunday was to be the veto power against endless war.

Crosby, Stills & Nash, Jackson Brown, Bonnie Raitt, the Eagles, Stevie Wonder, Linda Ronstadt and Donovan were some of the performers. I was given the role of handling stage left, where the performers entered and exited the stage. I'll never forget the experience of the sound wave of 106,000 people cheering when the curtain was opened and the wave rolled over the stage, knocking me back a step or two. I ducked out for a break and smoked a J with a few of the performers and speakers. Jeff Bridges, Max Gail and David Crosby were there. It was particularly nice to see Crosby healthy, with excellent musical chops and fine voice. I had last seen him a few years before and on that occasion I was greatly concerned for the life path he appeared to have chosen. Stevie Wonder's band Wonder Love was the true star of the day, although the Eagles were in fine form, too. Actually, all the performances were phenomenal and uplifting. The speakers between the musical acts were electrifying and dynamic, but none surpassed the succinct and articulate Patti Davis. Davis had written the lyrics to "Take It To the Limit," the Eagles career breakout song.

Patti Davis, President Reagan's daughter, was vehemently opposed to all of his inhumane policies and made a brief, brilliant speech in opposition. The short time I spent around her, however, left me with a grudging respect for her parents, because at the minimum they had endowed her with a mind of her own. Plus, I always appreciated her father's quote about horses: "There's something about the outside of a horse that's good for the inside of a man."

One reason all of the mega-talent agreed to show up was because the event would not be video-taped or recorded in any way, thus ruling out any future gain or profit from this historic occasion.

On Peace Sunday, I agreed to book a number of the groups to perform at one of my shows in Northern California. I was glad to get to meet the entertainers in person because a dark cloud had come over the music scene, a dark cloud called "free base." I was personally saved from this scourge by what I've always called the "Tibetan Cure."

I discovered the Tibetan Cure when I returned to Nepal to trek. I was informed that my trek sindar, Nymgyl, was a hopeless drunk. Big Red Ted described him as "a sad, disheveled and pitiful Navajo hanging around the outside of a reservation pawn shop begging for booze." Nymgyl had worked his way up to trek cook and then sindar (or head of the trek) on many of the major treks Ted and others had put together.

It shocked me to hear him badmouthed. He had married a lovely Tibetan girl and they had two children and a comfortable home in Bodnath. I went to his home to see for myself how he could have fallen into this drunken state. Amazingly, I found him stone-cold sober. The Tibetan lamas had taken him in and performed a ritual to save him from alcoholism. That ritual involved putttting powder, covered by wax the size of coins, on his chest while he reclined. Incense was burned, chants were invoked, bells played and prayers invoked. Then a High Lama with a candle came forth and swoosh, all three of the wax marks on Nymgyl's chest ignited in flame. The powder in the wax was gunpowder!

He said his depression came from the constant stream of stories from refugees about the sad situation in occupied Tibet. "The Chinese are turning women into prostitutes and using forced labor to kill off the men," he told me.

Nymgyl proudly showed me the circular scars left on his chest and expressed his great satisfaction of being cured of the alcohol problem. "The treatment was good luck," he concluded.

The Tibetan lamas' painful addiction cure stayed in the back of my mind from that point on. It was after a sold-out concert by David Crosby's solo band that I promoted, that the Tibetan Cure manifested itself again. The star of the show invited me onto his bus. The band's next show was in San Francisco. Before I could say no to "ride down with us," the bus was moving. "You'll be glad you're going," the rock star assured me, "cause, I'm going to turn you on to the next thing – THE NEXT BIG THING!"

Hey, a little party rolling toward San Francisco with a warm, generous and outstanding artist and some of his beautiful friends would be nice. However, it wasn't very long until I was shocked to see that this "next big thing" was conjured up by mixing this and mixing that in glass vials. It also included the use of a propane torch to smoke the concoction.

"Man, you've got to be a plumber to wanna smoke this," I joked with him. "Wouldn't you just rather enjoy a big fat J? We're in the heart of the emerald triangle," I gently suggested. He continued to profess its incredible properties as he mixed and cooked. Trying yet again to change the subject, while I figured out what

Karl Jay David David Crosby Tony Saunders

the hell was going on, I queried, "Where's the guys in the band?" Those guys were absolute virtuosos. One of the girls in the bus answered, "They got their own ride. They can't afford this kind of party. You've gotta have *hits* . . . this kind of party is expensive."

I still tried to persuade him that the bounties of the local finest would be most cool and mellow. My reluctance was answered, as one person after another sucked on a glass pipe. Just as my turn on the pipe approached, the tour bus abruptly swerved and the lovely lass who was holding the propane torch tripped and the torch flame burned right through my vest and shirt.

"Ow!" along with a few colorful expletives bellowed at full volume, and I never took that first puff. In fact, I began to conjure up an excuse to get off the bus ASAP.

Just as Nymgyl has his three scars, I still have my little deep-burned badge of good luck on my chest. I call it my Tibetan cure.

Chapter Fifty

"There's not a damn line in this law nowheres
that makes it illegal to kill a Chinaman."
JUDGE ROY BEAN (1823 – 1903)

WHERE AND WHEN THIS JOURNEY BEGAN
CALIFORNIA, 1970

Big Red Ted, Bill Wassman and I were friends at 19. We met in college. By the end of 1970, Ted was married to Cathy and Bill had married Patty. A year later Rebecca and I were madly in love and showed it. Cathy and Patty took an immediate liking to Rebecca. Both wives had failed at their attempts to hook me up with a girl – Patty with a co-worker and Cathy with a cousin – and were glad that their husbands' best friend was no longer a temp-

Ted
Bill
Jerry

tation magnet for the single lifestyle. Bill, ever the "artiste" and deeply in love with Patty, wasn't demonstrative. He felt he had to display aversion to anything conventional with a forced nonchalance, especially in matters of the heart.

The six of us left the United States for political exile. President Nixon was a rightwing nut case and everyone we knew was getting busted. Porsche Pete made a living fixing Porsches. He got two and a half years for trying to sell a couple of chunks of hash. Spade Johnny got eight years for trying to buy some hash. Dean the Dream – three years in a Spanish prison for possession of one gram. The first six months of his sentence found him in a 6' x 6' medieval dungeon. Generalissimo Franco ruled the Spain that gave such harsh sentences for such tiny infractions. Franco's draconian rule was maintained by putting lawyers in jail, show trials and torture.

Nixon's justice department went for the Franco model, big time. His own taped conversations would later reveal his disdain for citizens' rights and the rule of law.

On display in the Music and the Law Wing at the Rock and Roll Hall of Fame is a magazine article that demonstrates how the "arrest and intimidate lawyers" phase was implemented. The exposé article was published by "Rolling Stone" magazine, and you can thank your lucky-human-rights stars that it was. Joe Eszterhas, who went on to great Hollywood fame, wrote it. The article, entitled "Nark" was his first magazine assignment after newspaper reporting. Eszterhas' article is suitably embellished with rat illustrations to show its political leaning – informants, undercover narks and snitches are rats.

The centerpiece of the article is the description of a raid, by the state of California's highest ranking narcotics chief and Marin county's top agent (plus sixteen deputies) on an office-opening party for two long-haired lawyers who were less than a year out of law school. This home/office invasion in Marin is chronicled in detail in the Eszterhas article. We were all at that party.

The reason for all this attention lavished on two young lawyers, Mark Sussnow and "Handsome" Pat Herron, was likely due
to a famous informant named "Joe the Salamander" and the fact
that these two lawyers happened to defend people accused in pot
cases. As the record states, the Salamander said he "smelled marijuana" at the party and even though the eighteen officers never
found any drugs of any sort on the premises, they made fifty-two
arrests. A judge cut everybody loose by noon the next day. Three
legal heroes emerged from this dark, evil, politically motivated raid
– Patrick Hallinan, his brother Terence and Tony Serra.

Attorney Tony Serra would have his life and legal career en-
shrined in the movie "True Believer," the moving, nonfiction account of a man known to be innocent by the authorities and held
in San Quentin prison for nine years. A Korean-American from
a poor family, he was falsely imprisoned to cover up the heinous
crimes, including murder, committed by an informant for the
police. Tony Serra got him out of jail by exposing a government
operation that was designed to keep a vile thug such as this informant was, on the streets.

In the early '70s, Terence Hallinan was primarily known for
being Patty Hearst's first legal representation after she was freed
from her kidnappers and arrested by the FBI in San Francisco.
Hallinan's opening legal defense salvo was that Patty Hearst had
been brainwashed.

Patty Hearst had been held blindfolded in a closet for 45 days.
She had been sexually molested in that closet by the ringleader
of her captors, the Symbionese Liberation Army. It was a political
army with seven members. In her defense, part of what Terrance
Hallinan first offered was ". . . when the blindfold was removed she
felt as if she was on an LSD trip. Everything appeared so distorted
and terrible she believed and feared she was losing her sanity."
Hallinan was quickly removed as her attorney for this remark in
the middle of a very substantial and succinct defense. The hind-
sight of history and later acceptance of such psychological condi-

Photo by Annie Leibowitz Courtesy of *Rolling Stone* MAGAZINE

tions as the "Stockholm syndrome," would prove that he was on to something.

The third legal crusader was Patrick Hallinan. After the aforementioned raid, some legal case was cooked up against him. We never learned the details or wanted to.

None of these three was arrested the night of the raid because, earlier in the evening, Patrick Hallinan had knocked down the Assistant D.A. during an argument over certain devious and illegal tactics. The same "tactics" would shortly be occurring at this very party, that very night. Embarrassment over the fight caused the three lawyers and their wives, along with most other professional types, to leave the party, thus avoiding the bust. The incident did make the morning papers. The odd twist was that the Assistant D.A., after being clocked by Patrick Hallinan's right cross, did not say, "I threw a weak left hook that missed" or "I shoulda ducked." Instead, he left in a screaming huff, which could have been the impetus for Patrick Hallinan's 25-year problem.

San Francisco's famous society and gossip columnist, Herb

Caen, in his morning-after column in the San Francisco Chronicle, managed to add a certain humor to the *"affaire de legal"* that took place in the high rolling Marin hills. Herb Caen, as was his literary gift, gave his morning readers a chuckle:

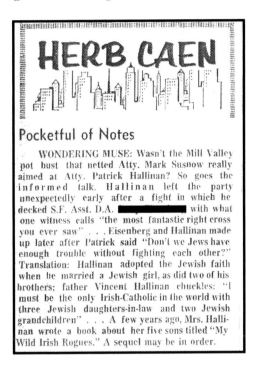

HERB CAEN

Pocketful of Notes

WONDERING MUSE: Wasn't the Mill Valley pot bust that netted Atty. Mark Susnow really aimed at Atty. Patrick Hallinan? So goes the informed talk. Hallinan left the party unexpectedly early after a fight in which he decked S.F. Asst. D.A. ████████ with what one witness calls "the most fantastic right cross you ever saw" . . . Eisenberg and Hallinan made up later after Patrick said "Don't we Jews have enough trouble without fighting each other?" Translation: Hallinan adopted the Jewish faith when he married a Jewish girl, as did two of his brothers; father Vincent Hallinan chuckles: "I must be the only Irish-Catholic in the world with three Jewish daughters-in-law and two Jewish grandchildren" . . . A few years ago, Mrs. Hallinan wrote a book about her five sons titled "My Wild Irish Rogues." A sequel may be in order.

It was not much of a laugh or even a chuckle (unless you consider gallows humor funny) for the fifty-two folks crammed into the two drunk tanks in the county jail. It wouldn't be funny for them – ever.

Two other items of importance that were not included in the light-hearted Chronicle column were: 1) it certainly takes longer than 20 minutes to assemble two of the state's top narks and the sixteen plainclothes men who happened to arrive at the party in such an untimely manner, as they did, shortly after the fight erupted; and 2) one of the young attorneys who co-hosted the party was the president of the San Francisco Federated Young Democrats organization.

Chapter Fifty-One

"In 1963, a band of beatniks arrived in Kathmandu. They were led by a man who had renounced his citizenship and believed that it was time to carry Western philosophy to the East. The crazy-wisdom of Jack Kerouac's "Dharma Bums" mixed with the romance-of-the-road view of Robert Lewis Stevenson, whose credo was: "It's the journey, not the destination." When they arrived, they set up their campground around a compound on the far reaches of the Valley. A runner was dispatched from the Palace. He invited the leader to have an audience with the King. The King thought they were a tribe of sadhus with long hair."

COUNTERCULTURE ORAL HISTORY

CALIFORNIA, SUMMER OF 1971

After the details of what had happened were pieced together, it seemed to us that it was time to find freedom somewhere else on the earth. All three of us had done the student backpacking youth-hostel-Europass-pass-train-last-class-Mediterranean-ferry trip. Bill and Ted had motorcycled across Europe and made it to Turkey. I traveled to Europe and left for Morocco to do some fantastic horseback riding near Fez. These traveling adventures were among the early, common bonds of our lasting friendship.

Ted insisted we all move to Kathmandu. He had been in the Peace Corps in India and after completing his obligation had spent some months in Nepal – "clean air, clean water and legal *charas*" chanted Ted.

Bill preferred the lush and peaceful Spanish island of Ibiza. He felt we could make a living as its tourism evolved from the "cheapskate-traveler trek" into a destination for the rich and famous. Only problems: Dean the Dream had left the Spanish islands for a Spanish jail; the governance of the island was questionable and would most likely not be hospitable to our freewheeling, adventurous spirit as long as Generalissimo Franco was alive; and, it looked like a designated regency might run the place in his name for another decade.

"Afghanistan," I chimed in. "Clean air, clean water, legal everything. There's even a money market I heard about where you can change any currency in the world for any other. Afghanistan has centuries of business on the old silk road." Also, I had really come to appreciate the freedom and lifestyle I felt the people of the Atlas Mountains enjoyed.

While Ted was in the Peace Corps in India, Bill had worked for Vista, the domestic Peace Corps (a code word for helping folks in the African-American part of town.) At the same time, I taught the poorest of the poor white kids in the Head Start program in rural white-bread America, where I encountered "dollar-an-hour dads," housing with outside plumbing and families accruing deep debt at the company store.

Our ladies had other things in common, besides falling in love with "adventurous sorts of guys," as they would say. All had attended a year of finishing school before going to college. Art, literature, dance and emotional maturity could be the reason they wanted men who were into action, not accounting; why they would rather boil well water and keep a cookfire going instead of living in bland suburbia. This was the broad, new horizon extolled by the woman's liberation movement.

Rebecca's mother and her four aunts were all college graduates and avid readers. The travel stories from the books they read were, in a sense, brought into reality through her. Her mother and aunts all wrote lengthy, intelligent letters, and for Rebecca it was almost like a daily diary because she had to answer so many. Cathy, Patty and Rebecca had been exposed to museums, Shakespeare, the great books, charitable works and church. Rebecca came from an open-minded, mixed Jewish-Presbyterian family.

Now all three had experienced a totalitarian, repressive, brutal action with the police. This was what they had been taught that life was like in a dark, repressive society or dictatorial, banana republic regime, not their beloved America! They openly professed to any and all during these emotionally distraught episodes that their men were idealists who wanted racial and religious harmony . . . hope for the less fortunate . . and an end to the endless war. The women wanted the same thing, too, and that was the beauty of it all; that, and a lot of loving. Their men were not criminals or dangerous, even in their thoughts. These men, like themselves, were clinging to the hopeful belief that love would rule the world. All war was wrong. The "Livin' Right and Being Free" axiom was one of America's best.

At the suggestion of Mark Susnow, the other lawyer who had been busted, Joe Eszterhas contacted us to be interviewed about the now infamous police action. Ted and I agreed because the interview was being written for "Rolling Stone" magazine, and we considered RS to be an un-co-opted bastion of truth. Plus, we basically didn't want to cut and run without a bit of hitting back through the media. After the interview in Mark's office, the partici-pants were sent to the apartment of a photographer just around the corner on Steiner Street to have pictures taken for the piece. The photographer was Annie Leibovitz. She posed Mark Susnow, holding her own phone and actively gesturing. She then snapped another of Pat Ryan looking "lawyerly tough." Terence Hallinan refused to be photographed. She had to grab a snap of Tony Serra, walking through City Hall. Her magnificently staged portrait of Patrick Hallinan, in front of a mural of Pancho Villa, gave the pub-lic a hint of her great artistic talent.

Ted is quoted in the Eszterhas "Nark" article that hangs in the Rock and Roll Hall of Fame: "People identified themselves as police and crashed through the door. At gunpoint, they herded us down to a lower bedroom. The attorney Pat Herron, co-host of the party, asked if they had a warrant and they told him to shut up. Fifty-two people herded into a bedroom.

None of the police was in uniform. Ted adds in the article, "When I first looked out of the bedroom I didn't believe they were police. I thought they were holdup men."

When the article appeared, Bill and Patty became so paranoid about the whole episode that for many years afterwards they asked all of us not to talk about it.

Big Red Ted is quoted one more time in the "Nark" article and, to us, this quote summed it all up: "Hey man, it's bad karma." The attempt at an Orwellian "Animal Farm" political takeover in the Nixon era of Agent Orange, the Napalm bombings, the policy of destroying villages in order to save them, COINTELPRO, and the "I don't need no stinkin' badges" mentality, all condensed into that one quote. Joe Eszterhas wrote it, "Rolling Stone" published it and

Bust In Marin
Dope Raid Called Political Attack By Young Demo

By Donovan Bess

Mark Susnow, president of the San Francisco Federated Young Democrats, said yesterday he was a victim of a "political attack" when narcotics agents invaded his Mill Valley home last December and arrested him on a marijuana charge.

The 25-year-old San Francisco lawyer and his wife, Susan, 21, were jailed on December 12 after a posse of state and Marin county narcotics agents broke into a housewarming party he was giving to celebrate a new law partnership with J. Patrick Dunn.

He said scores of respectable Bay Area notables, including "several deputy district attorneys," were at the party in his rustic Hillside home in the Marin woods.

Susnow and his wife were charged with possession of marijuana and maintaining a place where marijuana is used. But the charges were dismissed in San Rafael on Tuesday by Municipal Court Judge Peter A. Smith.

The raid was organized after an informant — who has an executive job in the Financial District here, according to Susnow — told police a few persons in the house were smoking marijuana.

Thirteen other persons, including the acting student body president of Hastings College of the Law, were jailed on charges of visiting a place where marijuana was present. They were released later "without prejudice."

"The whole thing was a political attack on me," Susnow told reporters, because he specializes in defending persons accused of violating the marijuana laws.

He said the raid was led by Gerriet von Raam of the State Bureau of Narcotics Control who, according to an affidavit from one guest, told Susnow: "I'm going to ruin your reputation."

The attorney said the agents broke down his door and searched for drugs in the house although the warrant they had was not signed by a judge.

"They came at about 1:40 a.m., placed me in handcuffs in my own house and kept me there until 3:30 a.m., not letting me make a telephone call," he asserted.

They got a search warrant from Superior Court Judge E. Warren McGuire at 3:50 a.m., court records in San Rafael showed.

The jurist later quashed his own warrant — and Tuesday Judge Smith threw out the case on grounds that the state had no evidence in view of the fact Judge McGuire had ruled his own search warrant was invalid.

But Michael Anthony in the Marin district attorney's office said yesterday he is appealing Judge McGuire's decision with the intent of retrieving evidence to proceed against the Susnows.

Van Raam said he had no comment in view of the fact that the case is under appeal.

AGENTS

Susnow said about 150 persons attended the open house at his rustic hillside home. He said that while he appreciated the need for narcotics agents to do their job well, "there is a need for overzealous agents to be checked."

"You don't know how this feels until it happens to you," he said. "We felt like we were being robbed."

ATTORNEY MARK SUSNOW AND HIS WIFE SUSAN
The case was dismissed Tuesday because of a faulty search warrant

the Rock and Roll Hall of Fame preserved it. It is a true metaphor for the "peace is at hand" administration that was secretly carpet-bombing peasants in Cambodia; and for America at that time, at the start of the dismal year of 1970. "Hey man, it's bad Karma."

Bill and Patty called in. They had done their research and found out that Ted was right when he said, ". . . the police in Nepal are allowed, by law, to carry a stick only 1.5 inches in diameter."

Ted's final appeal to us was based on his past pan-Asia point of view, emanating from the two years he invested as a Peace Corps volunteer in a south Indian village, trying to create hand-dug water wells. Afterwards, he enjoyed three months of absolute Nirvana roaming the Kathmandu Valley. Ted said "Buddhists live peacefully here with each other. The cops carrying little sticks. That's all they need. Crime is so infrequent that their guard dogs are 12" – high but that's because they only have to bite people on the ankle."

We all agreed – Kathmandu in the spring.

Chapter Fifty-Two

"Lightning strikes . . . maybe once . . . maybe twice . . .
Oh . . . and it lights up the night . . .
And you see your gypsy . . .
You see your gypsy . . ."
"GYPSY," FLEETWOOD MAC

Mahadev Mandin, Tripureswar, in Kathmandu, Nepal proclaimed: "To all earth planet kingdom global souls GOD VISHNU HAS VETO POWER! Advertise by Newspapers Magazines & Histories." – *His Imperial Majesty, The Great Global Emperor Vishousamrat Chakravarit Raja Almighty Dr. King God Vishnu Sri Panch Bodamaharaj Dhiraj Bhagvan Triloka Bir Bikram Shah Dev*

God Vishnu Global Dejure Military Dictator Patron of the Globe.

The man who made the above proclamation claimed he was from an ancestral heritage who generations before had ruled Nepal. Anyone who spent time in the Kathmandu Valley during the eighties heard him declare his entitlement. On May

3, 1981, he handed out a full-color laminated photo of himself with his worldly, spiritual view on the reverse side.

Two weeks later, Rebecca and I attended an art show at the Alliance Francaise in Bangkok that coalesced into a Rock and Roll Raj reunion. The colorful piece of laminate, costly by Asian standards, was a signpost and milestone that signaled cosmic changes in Nepal. It was also the cause of shared mirth for all of us who had been there when you could not purchase a turnip after dark.

The artist was Evelyne Drouot, a gifted Eurasian beauty. Evelyne was employed in an executive position in Bangkok and commanded a very good salary. She found her way into the scene by being a vivacious and gracious hostess. Her home was classic Thai style, situated on one of the last *klongs,* or canals, that remain in Bangkok, a city that had been, in the recent past, connected by many canals and known as the "Venice of Southeast Asia."

Evelyne raged around Bangkok with Captain David and Bad Ad. They encouraged her to host a party around her up-coming art show. Like the Christmas party in Goa ten years before, the May 19 art show was broadcast via the traveler's telegraph along the tetracycline trail.

A restaurant known as the White Piano was everyone's headquarters in Bangkok. Tent Tom and his Tibetan wife, Latchu, now had two children, and Tom, being ever the entrepreneur and innovator, had established this truly international restaurant. Tom's place was built in a style that was the opposite of Evelyne Drouot's classic, traditional home. During the Vietnam War, a small enclave of California-style ranch homes had been built, with swimming pools right out of the Hollywood Hills, to house American military officers.

Tom had converted one of the houses into a stylish watering hole that was named for, and built around, a white piano that had been on the premises when he purchased the building. A talented Thai lady wearing an evening gown played Chopin and Debussy. The Thais are famous for their unique cuisine and their insistance on sanitation and cleanliness. Tom melded first-class Thai cuisine, prepared by skillful local chefs, with the ambiance of a culturally based outpost in Asia serving up equal portions of gossip and travel info. Visa problems? Where to get gamma globulin shots? Good tickets for David Bowie or the Police concerts? Answers were always available at the White Piano.

Bill Wassman's reputation as a great travel photographer was ascending like a shooting star. He would willingly eat dog, roots or lizard and drink horrible homemade rotgut brew, if that was all there was available, just so he could get the photo that he wanted. To Bill, train station food was a step up from bus station food . . . if there was anything cheaper, Bill went for that.

Bill's photographs, and my creative descriptions of the joys of trekking, had established Big Red Ted's Humpayetti Trekking Co. as a destination. The unfortunate side effect was that Ted was now drawing a celebrity clientele. Ted said they loved the sunsets, they loved breathing the sweet mountain air, they loved jumping into those remote mountain lakes; they loved everything about trekking – except the walking part. Ted imitated their distress: "Who says this is fun, who said this is a good time? Get me a helicopter!!" Helicopter pickup cost five figures and ASAP for Ted's current clientele.

Ted's wife, Cathy, had developed a business around the traditional form of Tibetan weaving. It evolved into a fashion niche that employed a steady half-dozen Tibetan women. The finished product was more like a piece of art than wearing apparel.

The Shrimp was still his wildly-flamboyant self and a successful commercial photographer. His assignments were to take photographs of Western oil company executives shaking hands with local sheiks or members of the royal Saudi family. He admitted to acting more British by "curtseying with the best of them." He regaled us with tales of heaping plates of Caspian Sea caviar and buckets of Dom Perignon champagne. He had two beautiful, old-style side-by-side houses in his compound and installed his photography studio in one of them. He zoomed around Bangkok in his new BMW with tinted windows. He always had the most expensive "consort" on his arm, a Thai girl who would decorously and quietly observe, while politely sipping iced tea and uttering only an occasional, breathy "yes" or "no." He sought out these geisha-like women and it was his deep secret as to where he found them.

English Andy had established himself in both Kathmandu and Bangkok as an art and antiquities dealer extraordinaire. He was rock steady and had a superior business sense. He was a master researcher and debunker of counterfeit treasures.

German Ted was also living full time in Bangkok. His life had taken a complete turnaround to the "short hair, suit and tie" level. He had conceived a child with a Thai bar girl, married her and was forced into living the straight life as a wannabe international businessman with some hopeful, nefarious dealings on the side. His personality was so soured by this change that nobody could socialize with him. Tom had "86ed" German Ted from the White Piano Bar because of his volatile behavior, including abuse of his Thai wife.

Milan Melvin was unable to attend the reunion because he had worn out his welcome across much of Asia. He owed a small fortune to a Tibetan turquoise dealer. For a while he had lived on an estate upriver from Bangkok. He bought a 38' powerboat to ferry him and friends via the river. This was smart because Bangkok

Dutch Bob   Shrimp

traffic had become infamous for its congestion and pollution. In a couple of years, Milan was able to scam some Thai businessmen in a semi-precious stone deal. Unlike the non-violent Tibetans, he had to exit Thailand in fear for his life. He moved his operation to Sri Lanka and ripped off a consortium of gem dealers in Colombo. Rumor had it that they, too, had a price on his head. He was living in Bali and establishing what he hoped to be his biggest and best flim-flam scam ever.

Uncle Thampa was a legendary, fictional character of Tibet and the rascally hero of a series of Tibetan fables known as "The Tales of Uncle Thampa." The stories were all presented in a humorous and ribald fashion and, as if born to do it, Bad Ad captured the Tibetan brush stroke style that perfectly matched these fables. He translated and illustrated many of those stories, including, "Uncle Thampa Sells Penises to a Nunnery," a good example of the nature and flavor of these tales.

Dutch Bob was in town for the party. I hadn't seen him since the purloined 1000 pounds in Amsterdam. Bob tried hard to sell me on the idea that he had tapped into a gold mine, with a new mantra: "I'm too old go to my native Holland now, I can only be a bridge there for new, exciting ideas from Asia." His latest scheme was not based on spices, but involved escorting tour groups through the casinos of Macau. The tourists would then carry skimmed money back to Swiss banks. Bob thought I would be a good shepherd.

Two of the guys who came over to Asia five years earlier with Rebecca and me had never returned to the States. Cannon married a Thai teacher and he was teaching in a new, modern suburb outside of Bangkok. McGinnis married a Tibetan girl and was living in the Kathmandu Valley and had tapped into a business in Tibetan antiques and curios through his wife's family.

Buddy Lynn lived in Bangkok and was writing stories in English for Asian airline in-flight magazines, as well as travel articles for newspapers in Canada.

Captain David, wanted in India, could not attend but sent his best regards.

We shared news of others who weren't there.

Jittendra and Beth were living in an ashram in a remote South Indian village eating rice and *dhal* and meditating six hours a day. They had been doing so for eight years. He was learning to make intricate wooden string instruments in the ancient Indian style.

Will the Thrill was on the run from Interpol and was rumored to be living amongst the hill tribes of Laos or in wartorn, wide-open Kashmir.

Tory was released for good behavior after one year of her three-year prison sentence for the hashish disk art illegalities. She had taken her daughter, Guava, and gone to Dharamsala to continue her studies and reaffirm her life, accompanied by the Tibetan teacher she had trained with during her jail time.

Dean the Dream was not in attendance since he was facing ten years in a South African jail for having turned on a local miss to herb. She had shared her newfound joy with the wrong old friends who, for her and Dean the Dream's own good, had brought in a local pastor to convince them further. When that effort fell short, the pastor brought in the constables.

Well Fed Fred was rustling up Tibetan antiques, and, with Charmin' Carmen, was selling them in Los Angeles.

Sweet and Sour Sue was living in my Tibetan tent pitched in the garden up on Dirty Creek.

To all in attendance, Big Ted proposed a toast: "The cowards turned back, the unfortunate died along the way."

It had been a decade of political upheaval, serious illness, authoritarian intrigue and reckless love. Rebecca and I were in Bangkok, on our way back to California much later than usual, because I could no longer safely grow cannabis. The county that was home to the American colony of the Rock and Roll Raj had instituted a program of fixed-wing aircraft surveillance in its search for growing operations. Ours ended after hundreds of thousands of dollars of make-work money was allocated to support this latest marijuana war.

I had learned the valuable lesson that the entire world was run on the principle of Royal License. The English would have called the expatriates who were gathered in Thailand on this special weekend, "privateers." Privateers were created in Britain when the prevailing moral climate would not allow the English navy to raid other nation's ships. In the USA, money for this year's fixed-wing aircraft surveillance would eventually lead to armed military-like sweeps of future farms. Mentally I wasn't able to handle that kind of daily paranoia. I'd decided to plant ecologically perfect nut trees where once the mighty, rare strains grew, and all of my seedling trees were flourishing.

The puppies that Kachook sired were a delight and thriving at the ranch. We were most happy because my son was breathing the clean, salt air of a great little northern California beach town. He and William IX (William VIII and Aggie's son), were actually only a month apart in age and were growing up, Asian-style, like cousin-brothers. Knowing that William VIII would have been happy about his son's well-being was a warm feeling to share. Old friends are good for the soul.

There is nothing I know of that that can match the love of a parent for a child, but when two human beings find true love it's an energy-renewing experience, even for those who are there at its inception. Big Ted and Cathy, Rebecca and I, such long-time intimate friends unafraid to share deep emotions with each other, were happy to see a new love emerge that day. A lasting love affair developed between the photographer, Bill Wassman, and the artist, Evelyne. It was against the backdrop of this evolving devotion that made the gathering in Bangkok so exceptional.

Illustration: John Douglas Moran.

The slogan on the 1981 T-shirt was *"Three years before 1984"* because the government had funded and authorized fixed-wing aircraft to search the emerald triangle. That ended marijuana cultivation. Sadly, Bob Marly passed as well.

The "Epilogue"

"Every day, I try to understand the meaning of this line: 'Live your life without ambition. But live as those who are ambitious.' Do that and you discover the discipline of living an authentic life – and of living hard, as if each day counts."

Dr. Larry Brilliant

California, 1970

Hollywood decided to make a sequel to the movie documentary "Woodstock," complete with fake hippie bands, a fake hippie audience and people who were paid to attend "free" shows. Hollywood also must have decided that casting Wavy Gravy and the Hog Farm in the film would give it a veneer of "hippie" credibility. All this, to make a movie called "The Medicine Ball Caravan." The film actually made it to a few theatres and some songs turned out to be worth listening to on the soundtrack album. Wavy Gravy was in on the Ken Kesey acid trips and rode on the Hog Farm bus that traveled to the original Woodstock. In the documentary of that famous musical event, Wavy Gravy became famous for his on-camera Master of Ceremonies role. He proclaimed to the 400,000 in attendance – "don't eat the brown acid."

"Don't eat the brown acid" became one of the defining moments in the hugely successful documentary that immortalized the event. The Hog Farm was also well known for managing the medicine tent that tended to people who didn't get Wavy's message in time. Those already on drug bummers and bad trips, to use the slang of that era, were lovingly cared for by the earth mothers of the Hog Farm and the scenes of kindness and compassion played well in "Woodstock: The Movie."

The big bonus that Rebecca and I would take full advantage of, was that "The Medicine Ball Caravan" was to be shot in England, in an attempt to hype the movie as being a reverse British musical invasion!

Two things happened: a lot of "movieola" money and a need for San Francisco hippie-looking people to fly to London and watch the bands perform in a park that had been rented for the production.

It's nice when they have big budget.

Rebecca and I got in on the fun as movie extras for the free plane tickets over to London and the $200 bucks cash promised to be paid upon arrival. We were promptly paid and within 48 hours we were on the cheapest Air India red-eye special on our way to Goa before the faux concert.

Looking back on it all, it might have been a mistake to leave the new friendships we'd made with some of the Hog Farmers, because they would enjoy an adventure rivaling anything that Kerouac or Hemingway ever chronicled.

Setting up a raffle, the Hog Farmers purchased a bus in London so they could drive to the country then known as East Pakistan, where there had been an incredible natural disaster. Flooding inundated the entire country and the resulting diseases killed an estimated quarter of a million people.

Unknowingly, the great reward that Hollywood fostered on the world was a successful medical fight against smallpox and preventable blindness in some of the most remote and desperate areas of the planet.

Dr. Larry Brilliant and his wife had emerged as the spiritual heads and guiding forces of the Hog Farm organization. Dr. Brilliant had proved his bonafides not only to the movie crew, but also to the Hog Farmers by taking advantage of an opportunity to address his fellow doctors at the American Medical Association. He bluntly stated, for public consumption, that the organization should be called the "American Murders Association." Once you've done something like that, why not join the Hog Farm?

Thus the Hog Farm's energies were directed toward assisting the victims of flooding in that horrendous human disaster. Money was pooled, a benefit was held in London and a bus was purchased.

The Hog Farm bus moved through Amsterdam, where they received free passes, and were asked to help with security at a Rolling Stones gig. Dovetailing with their fame in the Woodstock movies, the Rolling Stones gig gave them a lot of publicity on the European continent. Next, the Farmers were invited to the French-American Friendship Cultural Center in Paris. The Hog Farm turned that staid old edifice into a madcap party by smoking joints and jumping naked into the club's ornate swimming pool. The ensuing high jinks also brought them a great deal of European television attention, so when they passed through Germany they were able to put together a huge "acid-test" type event that enabled them to acquire a nearly new Mercedes-Benz luxury travel bus as well as money for the flood relief in East Pakistan.

The party/benefit was held in a city park in the great tradition of the Golden Gate Park events in San Francisco, where the participants routinely and proudly cleaned up after themselves. The clean-up portion of the tradition did not quite translate to Europe and when Dr. Larry Brilliant saw, at the crack of dawn, the thousands of left-over party kids, he wisely ordered a quick exit out of town.

Hog Farmers Milan Melvin, Well-Fed Fred and Tom Glenn did most of the driving. Calico, Wavy Gravy's wife, Bonnie Jean, and Peter Grimm made major contributions to getting the group across the not-always-easy-to-transit Middle East.

The imminent breakout of the India/Pakistan war thwarted their plans to go to East Pakistan and impelled them to get across the Indian border as fast as they could and head to Kathmandu. Flood relief would have to wait, but the seeds were planted and unexpected good karma would ensue. Meanwhile, Rebecca and I were on our way to Nepal.

Ted and Cathy, Bill and Patty, Bad Ad, English Andy, Will the Thrill and Sweet & Sour Sue were among the hardy few already living in Nepal when we arrived. Ironically, Sweet & Sour Sue had bailed on her relationship with Tom Glenn in Germany, found a new boyfriend and convinced him that the East was best. She had flown into Kathmandu before she had any idea that the Hog Farm bus would take a sharp left turn and wind up in that special place, too.

We were all living in a variety of old-style Nepalese homes with names such as "The Broken Yantra" and "The Double Dorje." These houses were built with ceilings that were only five feet five inches high and they had incredible, carved wooden doors and windows that were created by local artisans 150 years earlier. The homes had rudimentary kitchens and no indoor plumbing. They were as drafty and dank as any old English castle of yore.

At this time in Nepal, the Kathmandu Valley literally ran out of food at least once a day. There was not a turnip left in the stalls by 7:00 o'clock at night. Only when trucks laden with provisions started rolling out of the southern, warmer farm areas, and made the climb up to the mountainous capital city, did food appear in the markets again. Lack of luxuries did not diminish the magic and mystery that was, to us, another form of sustenance. No one yearned for frozen food and there always seemed to be chai flowing.

When Ted and Cathy, Bill and Patty, and Rebecca and I were living in Kathmandu along with fourth-generation Peace Corps workers, the Hog Farmers, and a few diplomats, the "Encyclopedia Britannica's" 1970 edition stated that the annual yearly income for a Nepalese was $200 U.S. dollars per year.

Road money was instant salvation to the Tibetan refugees of the Kathmandu Valley. The Tibetans just needed a capitalistic push and they ran with the ball. Tibetan carpet money enabled big brick apartment buildings to be built all over Bodnah. Boinah, in a remote corner of the Kathmandu Valley, was the home of one of the world's most ancient and holiest stupas. It was a natural place for the Tibetans to migrate when they fled the Chinese Communists. Slowly, Tibetan carpet money fueled the commercial take-over of the Swayambunath corner of the valley as well as the Thamal section of downtown Kathmandu. These economic inroads into the existing Newar commercial establishments were unheard of before the arrival of the Tibetans. The Newars had been the business elite for five hundred years before the Tibetans cracked the market place.

Western travelers from that era also contributed to the economies of the Nepalese, the Thais, the Balinese, the Burmese and any place that their traveler's checks or Western currency was spent.

Road people employed tailors in Pakistan and Thailand, stone masons in Bali, sari and silk makers in India and Turkoman rug merchants. Any money injected into these poor economies by anyone for any reason was tremendously appreciated. For example: The official exchange rate in Burma was six local to one U.S. dollar. The black market rate was nearly one hundred local to one U.S. dollar. In Rangoon, the guy you got the black market rate from operated near the river water taxis. He was an old Indian gentleman held over from the British Raj's rule. He was known as "the Man with the Teeth of Gold."

And, of course, some of the Westerners kept hand-press hash babas happy and supported the owners of many an opium den.

The Hog Farm bus delivered Dr. Larry Brilliant to Nepal, and he was living in a Himalayan monastery when he was hired to work for the World Health Organization smallpox program in New Delhi. He immediately became aware of the dire medical problems in Asia and was a leader of the team responsible for eradicating smallpox in Asia. Dr. Brilliant also began working on a cure for preventable blindness in the Himalayas and founded, along with Wavy Gravy, the Hog Farmers, and the Grateful Dead, the SEVA

Foundation. SEVA has restored sight to more than two million blind people in India, Nepal and Tibet.

Travelers came to Asia for many reasons – the adventure, the spiritual discovery, the romance, the exotic culture, the sex and drugs. What you found depended on who you were. Many became sick or scared and left after only a few days. Others found teachers, masters or gurus. Many were stimulated to create great artistic works and pursue scholastic endeavors. Many more brought home stories and inspired others to follow their paths across the continents. The Tibetans say that the diaspora of their culture was predicted and that the dharma, the teachings, the truth, even their medicinal lore, would be brought to the West in this way and hopefully, preserved.

As for us, we traveled to Europe with the maddest of the madcap hippies, happened to land in Goa, where, shortly thereafter, my sweetheart and I lived the life – from Amsterdam to Afghanistan, from the Northern California foothills to the high Himalayas of Nepal, from Indonesia to Jamaica. Our days of wild adventure and our nights of watching full red moons sink into shimmering, placid seas were as inevitable as breathing.

What is necessary to create an extraordinary, ten-year journey? For me, it's this: Rare air and the seldom seen. Great friends. A faithful dog and a strong, swift stallion. Secret beaches. Lost canyons with sparkling waterfalls. The birth of a child. A loving romance and, above all, the feeling of spiritual and personal growth at the end of that decade-long, over-the-rainbow, road.

Where Are They Now?

There are now over 700 smoke shops in Holland.

It is estimated that the marijuana industry in California produces revenues of over a billion dolars a year.

Big Red Ted: Brought and introduced the Dalai Lama to the United States Congress, 1991. Passed away, 2004.

Cathy Worcester: Lives in Kathmandu.

Bill Wassman: His photographs appear in many books. His work "Buddhist Stupas of Asia" was published in 2003. Passed away, 2003.

Patty Wassman Miller: Works with Doctors Without Borders.

German Ted: Killed with his son in a motorcycle accident in Bali, 1986.

Tory Wells: Passed away in 2006. She was estranged from her daughter, Guava, and survived by two sons.

Rebecca: Lives in Northern California.

Shashi Kapoor: Continues to appear in major international cinema.

Jennifer Kapoor: Passed away on Sept. 7, 1984.

Tent Tom and Lachu: Have two grown children and live in Southern California.

Well Fed Fred: Passed away in 2001.

English Andy: Married, with children, in Thailand.

Skipper Gary: Boat captain in Hawaii, raising his daughter Erin.

Dr. Brilliant: Board of Directors, SEVA Foundation for preventable blindness. Director, Google Foundation.

Wavy Gravy: Works for many humanitarian causes; was an ice cream flavor for a decade or so. Developed Camp Winnarainbow for underprivileged kids.

The Sizzler: Unknown.

Montreal Michael: Somewhere on the Seven Seas.

Captain David: Married, spends time between his estate and a large yacht in Monaco.

Sweet-and-Sour Sue: Lives in Bali.

Archie: Lives in Seattle.

Patrick Hallinan: Practices law.

Terence Hallinan: San Francisco District Attorney for two terms, now in private practice.

Tony Serra: Practices law.

Jerry Garcia: Passed away, 1995.

Mountain Girl and her daughters: Going strong.

Tarthang Tulku: Prolific author, established Nyingma Institute and Dharma Publishing.

The Shrimp: Commercial photographer in Thailand.

Evelyne Wassman: Lives in New York City.

Mona and Momma: whereabouts unknown.

Mark Susnow: Life Coach, lives in Northern California.

Charmin' Carmen: Married with two children in California.

Bad Ad: Lives in Nepal.

Aggie: Lives in Northern California.

Howard Wales: Phobic. Performs rarely.

Jittendra: Re-married with two children. Lives in Hawaii. Continues to make and market high quality Indian stringed musical instruments.

Beth: Lives in Maine.

Milan Melvin: Passed away in 2002.

Dutch Bob: Passed away 2004.

Alejandro: Killed in an automobile accident in Spain.

Dean the Dream: Seen or heard of in South Africa, Australia and Prague.

"Rabid" Rakow: In 1981, Ron Rakow allegedly to have disappeared with 2.5 million dollars stolen from the Church of Scientology. He is wanted by Interpol.

Ghiaz: Joined the *mujahadeen* to fight the Soviets in Afghanistan.

Charles "Serpentine" Sobhraj: Released from jail in India after twenty years. He was tried for the murders in Nepal and currently in prison there.

The original sensimilla T-shirt (1974) and the Bohda Yogi

In researching "Where Are They Now?," Joe Petrie sent me the following remembrance he wrote about Will the Thrill, specifically; but many who are mentioned in the preceding "Where Are They Now" list were there on this day.

The Durga Puja is the largest and most bizarre festival in Nepal and goes on for fifteen days. On the night of the eighth day, called Kal Ratri, the ritual sacrifices begin. At every Durga temple in Nepal many buffalo and goats are sacrificed and their blood is poured over the statues of the goddess Durga. This is the day the Goddess Durga conquered all evils. On the ninth day, Vishwas Karma, the god of creativity is worshiped. All moving machinery is blessed by blood, including vehicles and airplanes. Many more buffalo and goats are sacrificed and their blood smeared to get the blessing and protection from the Goddess Durga against any accident for one year.

On that ninth day, Will the Thrill had a luncheon smorgasbord and vehicle round-up party for a trip to the Dakinkali temple to witness this Dashin festival in festive fashion. Most attendees lived in Bohda, a small village that encircled the huge Bodnath Stupa, the oldest and holiest Buddhist shrine in Nepal. A Yogi lived at the entrance of the Bodnath Stupa and smoked hashish chillums to Lord Shiva daily. Many a traveler, ex-pat or pilgrim smoked with him. He not only spoke English very well, but the Yogi would teach various meditation and Yoga practices to any that asked. The Yogi claimed he could make himself lighter than air and meditate with his special breathing technique. His picture had been taken by so many people over the years that he had a portfolio of photos of himself in different Yogic positions. Will the Thrill made sure the Yogi boarded one of the recently blessed, blood-splattered vehicles.

I remember it being an overcast and humid day when we arrived at the Dakinkali Temple. We laid out a rug and some sat in a circle and smoked a chillum of Nepalese hash. Others tried to pick up something spiritual, special or unusual.

Animal after animal was slaughtered in frenzy and their blood splashed on the statue of the Goddess Durga. Once slaughtered, the carcasses would be taken to the stream and further butchered and rinsed. The stream was already red when we arrived. Our nostrils caked from the blood in the air.

Will the Thrill was boisterously enjoying his party by trying to out smoke the Yogi. The Yogi was amazing. He could take more smoke in one hit than any Westerner. The ever unfolding ritual is loud. Drums are beating. Women are trilling and many charas babas line the slopes to the blood red waters.

Suddenly the Yogi got up from the carpet and walked to the stream. At the edge he sat in lotus position and put each foot behind his head. He stood on his hands. The Yogi then turned his body upside down and walked on his hands into the stream. He began doing a deep-breathing technique and then suspended himself on only one hand. And then . . . on none! The Yogi was suspended in air. He calmly put one hand down and then the other and walked out of the stream upside down. He walked up the slope to a lot of awestruck and silent observers.

The Yogi smiled.

The letter above was written and posted from Kabul, Afghanistan, by Sharon Zarkin to her mother, Sylvia.

The photo was taken in 1969 behind the Matchbox hotel in Kathmandu. Sharon, on drum, is accompanied by Om Eric on flute. The ganja plant in the background is growing wild behind the hotel.

Sharon traveled to many of the countries mentioned in this book although she is not part of this story. She put in many hours towards its publication.

Sharon said: "I never met Bill Wassman that I know of but, like him, I lived a long time in New York City and it can make you hard. Bill is said to have commented about Asia: 'If you weren't careful,

you got sick. If you weren't *really* careful you died.' With this I agree."

"He also said, 'When you're ready to strangle them it's time to leave.'"

JERRY BEISLER has had three books of poetry published: *Hawaiian Life and the Pink Dolphins*, *St. Elvis and Missionary Thought* and *Mother Asia and Cousin California*. He has also published international political commentary, travel articles, historical research, film and video reviews, and short stories.

Beisler attended Indiana University, Mexico City College and San Francisco State University.

As the Prayer Wheel Turns
THE SERIES:

The Sixties: *Hoosiers and Hippies*
The Seventies: *The Bandit of Kabul*
The Eighties: *Cocaine Cowboys*
The Nineties: *Paradise, Pain and Production*

Special Thanks Contribution: Kate Anderson and Julie Bowers

Bandit of Kabul Photo Credits

Front Cover (Author's Photograph): taken with an old-style box camera by a local photographer who took pictures of pilgrims to the Blue Mosque.

Back Cover Photograph: Janice Popper.

Bill Wassman was a professional photographer. Any photos he took in this book were only snapshots.

Additional photo credits: M. Barrish, B. Ciz, G. Keeproth, Shelia Agnew, Sam D'Aloisio, Tom Borreli, Patty Nelson, Earthman Mur for the Goa party, Kay Caldwell, Hans Daumer, Sue Lawing, Bruce Puterbaugh, Ron Rakow, Tory Welles, John Stanton, Steve McGuiness, Peter Cannon, Capt. David, Bad Ad, Steve Nash, Dennis Hartford, Fred Mendoza and Tibetan mastiff puppy by Nymgyl.

T-Shirt photos: Mike Craycraft.

I used a Kodak 110 and shot in black and white, the only film available in Asia.

Unless noted, all art work on or in this book was created by Andrew Annenberg, www.AndrewA.com.